W0246673

CRICKET
Drona

CRICKET
Dro*n a*

For the Love of Vasoo Paranjape

ESSAYS BY
SACHIN TENDULKAR,
SUNIL GAVASKAR,
RAHUL DRAVID
AND OTHER
CRICKETING GREATS

JATIN PARANJAPE
ANAND VASU

EBURY
PRESS

An imprint of Penguin Random House

EBURY PRESS

USA | Canada | UK | Ireland | Australia
New Zealand | India | South Africa | China | Singapore

Ebury Press is part of the Penguin Random House group of companies
whose addresses can be found at global.penguinrandomhouse.com

Published by Penguin Random House India Pvt. Ltd
4th Floor, Capital Tower 1, MG Road,
Gurugram 122 002, Haryana, India

Penguin
Random House
India

First published in Ebury Press by Penguin Random House India 2020

Anthology copyright © Jatin Paranjape 2020
Copyright for individual articles vests with respective authors

All rights reserved

10 9 8 7 6 5 4 3

The views and opinions expressed in this book are the authors' own and the
facts are as reported by them which have been verified to the extent possible,
and the publishers are not in any way liable for the same.

ISBN 9780670092154

Typeset in Adobe Caslon Pro by Manipal Technologies Limited, Manipal
Printed at Replika Press Pvt. Ltd, India

This book is sold subject to the condition that it shall not, by way of trade
or otherwise, be lent, resold, hired out, or otherwise circulated without the
publisher's prior consent in any form of binding or cover other than that in
which it is published and without a similar condition including this condition
being imposed on the subsequent purchaser.

www.penguin.co.in

This is a legitimate digitally printed version of the book and therefore might not
have certain extra finishing on the cover.

This book is dedicated to all the coaches who empower young players and enable them to truly believe in themselves in their crucial formative years. Such coaches selflessly commit to helping young players reach their potential and get on the big stage under bright lights, while themselves staying very far from where those lights are shining . . .

'All my life I've been attached to the game of cricket, and even now I keep learning something new from it—something fascinating, interesting and worthwhile. I have coached for several years, and the talent that I now see emerging is very impressive. However, most youngsters play to get something out of this great game, and their experience is devoid of pleasure and humour; I feel the game is the poorer for it. Pleasure and humour play a great part in uplifting the spirits on the field. The humorous banter and jokes exchanged during a match remain forever etched in one's memory.'

'The competitive spirit minus the stress and the tension is always more healthy, both for the youngsters and for the game. But these days, more than necessary importance is given to quantity—to numbers—than to quality. I have always felt that quantity breeds mediocrity.'

'I most happily maintain that if one has played cricket in the right spirit, one can face life more easily, because cricket has more fluctuations, more ups and downs, than life has.'

'Cricket is a funny game. One day you will be on the pinnacle of success, and on the next day you may be down into an abyss. Hero one moment and zero the next.'

'Your game reflects your character. While playing, you face different situations at different times, and everyone responds to these differently.'

'Cricket, as is the case with so many other fields of life, is changing its character. There have been advances in technique over the years, more so in bowling technique. The emergence of aerobics instructors, gym trainers, yoga teachers, dieticians, physiotherapists, and sport psychologists has brought about significant change. Player behaviour is monitored. Cameras and the third umpire further ensure fair play. Despite all this, however, the glorious uncertainty of this game has reigned supreme, and thank God for that!'

—Vasoo Paranjape

Contents

Foreword

Ifirst met Vasoo at the Dadar Union ground for a
Purshottam Shield match. It was my first time playing
for Dadar Union, and I was in the reserves. So I had
ample time to watch and observe him and the other DU
players, as well as to absorb the culture and ethos of this
wonderful club.

Soon after, I was playing under him, and he would take
me aside for small chats that helped me immensely. There
was no technical advice as such but little astute observations
after every game about how I batted and, more importantly,
about how I could have batted.

He had the wonderful ability to spot some error and
communicate it to you in a direct but humorous way.
What this did was to allow the player—while helping him
understand what needed to be done to rectify a fault—to
also laugh at his own mistakes. And because Vasoo's style
was humorous, you repeatedly thought about what he'd
said and remembered it. Its impact was always positive, as

it made every player believe that he could become better by eliminating a fault.

Being at Dadar Union meant you knew that the game was always bigger than the individual, and that the team always came first. It also taught you discipline; even the biggest of players would be dropped if they turned up late to the ground.

Vasoo was always first at the ground, and with an amused look on his face he would watch the other team members report for the day's match. As you walked up to him, he would heartily say good morning, addressing you by name and that made you feel special. After the game there would invariably be a discussion on the day's play, and then about cricket generally, so nobody left for another good hour or so.

Dadar Union taught you a lot, including little things like the importance of having proper cricketing attire—we were always told that we must look like cricketers. We were taught unstinting discipline and underlying it was a respect for the game. From taking care of your kit and keeping it clean, to pure cricketing things—such as backing up for a throw, shouting for a high catch, calling out for an extra run, dragging the bat in the crease—Dadar Union drummed this into you, and we were all led by Vasoo.

Dadar Union was a champion team. It had class batsmen, terrific bowlers and top fielders. Vasoo himself was one of the very best fielders and though he didn't get many batting opportunities, whenever he did he would take the team to a win.

There was one innings in particular, against traditional rivals Shivaji Park Gymkhana. We were in a perilous position. Padmakar Shivalkar and Ramakant Desai were creating havoc with the ball when Vasoo went out and blasted them all over the ground. He won the match for us, accompanied by the last batsman.

The camaraderie and mateship at Dadar Union—it's hard for me to explain it. You had to be there and you had to have experienced it to understand how genuine it was. The other thing was that everyone at Dadar Union had a nickname. Mine—Sunny—was given to me by Vasoo and has stuck for life.

Vasoo loves Australian cricket. He just loves the positive, aggressive approach that the Aussies have shown over the years. And, of course, Sir Don Bradman was God for him.

He went with the Cricket Club of India team to Australia in 1972 and while most of the matches were in New South Wales, he was not going to leave Australia without meeting Sir Don in Adelaide. When asked if he was going to meet Sir Don, he replied with his usual sense of humour: 'How can one come to heaven and not meet God?' That's how much he loved Australia and Sir Don.

Later on, when I introduced Vasoo to Ian Chappell, they got on like a house on fire. They both love the game passionately, can talk about it endlessly and have millions of stories to tell.

On my second trip to Australia as vice-captain of the Indian team, Vasoo told me that if I met Sir Don I shouldn't leave his side even for a second. I was told, 'Observe everything, remember what he says, take notes.' I was supposed to share those details with Vasoo on my return.

On that tour, we were at a dinner reception hosted by the South Australia Cricket Association, and I was sitting next to Sir Don. I sat and listened to the great man as he talked about the 1947–48 Indian team and about his correspondence with Vijay Merchant and Russi Mody. He also asked me questions about the Shiv Sena and other things India. He said he regretted not having stepped out on to the deck to wave at the thousands of Indian fans who had gathered quayside just to get a glimpse of the great man when the ship carrying the Australian team to England had docked in Mumbai in 1948.

Vijay Merchant had gone and met Bradman on board the ship, but his request—that Sir Don come to the deck and wave to the fans—was turned down. Sir Don did not venture out of his cabin for the entire duration the ship was at the Mumbai port. He explained that his health was fragile, and he did not want to risk catching an infection. So he stayed put in his cabin.

Through the course of that dinner in Australia, I had been having a strong urge to go to the toilet but kept remembering Vasoo's instruction not to leave Sir Don's side even for a second. So I waited and waited, and much after the dinner was over, an SACA official took Sir Don aside for a chat. It was then that I allowed myself a break!

There was plenty to learn from Sir Don about the Indian cricket team of 1947–48. But on that evening, I also learnt from him how to sweep bread crumbs from the top of a table to the palm of your hand before transferring them to a quarter plate. For some reason, that memory has stayed with me ever since.

Then, on the following tour in 1980–81, when I was the captain of the Indian team, Sir Don popped into our change room to meet the team. But I missed him. I was standing next to the sightscreen, as I wanted to see how a couple of our batsmen were shaping up against the South Australian pacers, led by Rodney Hogg. When Vasoo found out that I had missed meeting Sir Don, he did not let me hear the end of it. That's Vasoo and his veneration of Sir Don.

And, to put it simply, that's Vasoo and his love of the great game of cricket.

Mumbai   Sunil Gavaskar

Preface

I started reading poetry recently. My mother, an English professor of long-standing eminence, suggested that I read Francis Palgrave's poetry anthology *Golden Treasury*, and I must admit to having thoroughly enjoyed it. But the poems I read also made me think about the game I love, cricket. For example, these lines by the English poet Thomas Gray: 'To chase the rolling circle's speed/ Or urge the flying ball . . .' Reading *Golden Treasury* made me realize, yet again, that cricket is not just a game to me but is very much the driving force of my life. Everything, even poetry, reminds me of cricket.

I have always loved the game. There are pictures of me aged seven or eight with a bat in hand, standing ready to face the ball in a Chanderpaulesque stance, very square-on, feet all over the place. That I would play cricket for nearly twenty years of my life was a foregone conclusion to many, including myself. Very soon, I was attending selection trials for my school team at Don Bosco.

One fine day, after school, when I was playing with my classmates, I was summoned by the school's cricket coach, Kumar Tamhane, a sturdy man of few words who always wore a fur hat. He called me aside and asked me to attend practice the next day. I ran home as hard as I could and reported the news to my father, who said rather keenly that I should go with him to get a bat and a pair of gloves as I was left-handed and Don Bosco did not have a left-hander in the squad. Batting would have been an issue the next day without an adequate pair of gloves. I was used to hitting a rubber ball with my friends in the school quadrangle, but facing up to a talented bunch of bowlers and playing with a hard, red ball was a different story altogether.

Still, the trial went fine, and a week later I was playing the Harris Shield, as an eleven-year-old in an under-17 competition. I batted rather well in my first match, or so I thought, before getting run out for 5. I had run diagonally to avoid an unusually long follow-through of the bowler and hence had to cover more than the twenty-two yards. My father was watching the game, with cricketers Anil Joshi and Avi Karnik, and in his inimitable style he told me that running straight might save me the next time.

My early years in the sport, at Hemant Hadkar's nets at the Matunga Gymkhana, were most memorable. I wore shoes given to me by Dilip Vengsarkar. The shoes were at least three sizes too big, and I had to put on three to four pairs of socks with them. I also remember that he gave me a Gunn and Moore bat with which he'd scored a few Test centuries. Only the middle of the bat carried the red ball marks—such was the quality of his batsmanship.

My father would often drop by and watch me play. I knew he was a very good player, and he was widely known as one of the best captains in Mumbai never to have actually led Mumbai.

Those were the years when I went to watch Dadar Union matches with my father. I have so many lovely memories, of sitting in tents at Cross Maidan and Azad Maidan; in the pavilions of the P.J. Hindu Gymkhana and Parsi Gymkhana; in the corner of the pavilion at the Cricket Club of India. We watched intently as Dadar Union rolled over the opposition, one team at a time. Dadar Union was always aggressive, always meticulous, always playing as a team, always enjoying the game, always playing hard, always fielding brilliantly, always playing for the love of the game.

I also started becoming a fan of my father. I loved the way he would be dressed for a game, in his creams, a cravat around his neck and a cigarette invariably hanging from the corner of his mouth as he adjusted the cravat to perfection. I saw him leading the team, I saw him scoring runs, I saw him getting out cheaply, I saw him fielding brilliantly at point or at backward short leg. I saw him with his troops and saw how affectionately he interacted with them. He had genuine respect for their talent and genuine love for the game. He had a razor-sharp vision, a knack for strategy and tactical execution, which he brought to each match.

There were, of course, the Thursday evening meetings when the entire team would descend on our house to plan for Sunday's game over cups of steaming tea and snacks made by my mother. I would always, always be around and would drop everything for that hour or so. I would listen attentively

to the plans being laid out, the scenarios being envisaged, the
SWOT analysis being conducted. And then, on Sundays, I
saw all of it being played out seamlessly.

I once read that Mark Knopfler could be found sleeping
with his guitar after the rest of the band members left the
studio for a night of revelry. I saw nothing but that dedication
in my father's approach to the game. It was pure love being
played out, over and over again. Pure love and nothing else.
He revered this great game, not for what it had or hadn't
given him but for what it was. For what it is.

Anyone who has spent five minutes watching cricket
with my father will know what I mean. Where you and I
would see a contest between bat and ball, he sees a metaphor
for life. Where you'd see a bowler trying to get the best of a
batsman, he sees the questions that every man and woman is
faced with in life. Where you'd see a batsman trying to first
protect his wicket and then score runs when possible, he sees
the process of problem-solving, of addressing a challenge
and overcoming it.

For him, cricket was life and life was cricket. A dedicated
family man with an abiding love for his wife and nothing
but care and concern for his children, my father still lives for
cricket. As a child, this never bothered me because he had
more than enough love to give—both to us and to the game.

All his ideas resonated with me. 'Team above self' became
my mantra. I once read an interview of Michael Atherton,
where he said that he would like to be remembered as a
Lancashire batsman more than as an England captain. That
was the code by which my father also celebrated this game
and his lifelong relationship with Dadar Union.

These days, life seems to be only about success, money, fame and all the trappings that come with them. Sportspersons, too, have fallen prey to this myopic pursuit, and I have seen so many cricketers equate an IPL contract with success. Their love of the game seems to have dwindled, just as the generosity of the coaches—their desire to give— has become a thing of the past.

That's what this book is about: celebrating a man who made it his life's mission to give the gift of his wisdom to as many cricketers as he could reach out to; a man whose mission it was to identify talent, nurture it and strategically place it in the best pathways and in the best hands, so it could soar as high as possible.

His single-minded aim was to watch and appreciate the game for its beautiful nuances, the subtleties it revealed to those who cared to look, and to comment on the game in a way that enriched the knowledge of people listening to his critique. My father not only nurtured players, he nurtured cricket fans, inspiring them to become followers and lovers of this great game.

There haven't been many like him, and I, in all humility, feel that his story needs to be told, so that more people out there could be made aware of his unique vision of the game. If this book inspires anyone to think more deeply about the game—about why we play it, why we watch it, comment on it, cry over it, feel the highs of victory and the lows of defeat—that would be a fair reward for me.

I may be my father's greatest fan, but I know it for a fact that I am not his only admirer. In all my time in cricket, I have never met a person whose path has crossed with my father's and who has not been the better for it. That's just the kind of man he is. With a wink and a smile, with an arm around your shoulder, he will walk with you awhile. If you need a guiding hand, you won't have to ask. If you need to be left alone, he doesn't need to be told. If you need a pat on the back, a sympathetic shoulder, a hug or a handshake, there isn't a better man in the game than my father. Nobody gave so much to this game without once pausing to ask what he might get in return. In a sense, this book is only an extension of that philosophy. In every story recollected here, in every account that traces a passage of his life, there is a reflection of my father's heart and soul. And I feel fortunate to be able to share this with you.

Jatin Paranjape

Introduction

'Cricket coach is what I do; it's not who I am.' This was Eric Simons, the former South African fast bowler and the Indian team's bowling coach from 2010 to 2012. What he meant was that while he put a lot into being a coach, it was not something that defined him completely. And it remains a fact that Simons, who runs a large and successful construction-related business in South Africa, is so much more than just a cricket coach.

Now consider Vasoo Paranjape. He is a man of varied interests. He can hold forth on an array of subjects and that ensures he is always the life of the party. But when he speaks about cricket, he is a sight to behold. His eyes come alive, his heart is in every sentence he speaks and his words fight with each other to get out into the world. Like Simons, Vasoo Paranjape is not just a cricket coach. He is much more than that. In some ways, he is cricket in itself. He is everything that is good and great about the game.

It was at one of Chennai's smaller cricket grounds that I had the privilege of first meeting Vasoo Sir, more than two decades ago. He was coaching a team of youngsters from the National Cricket Academy in a Buchi Babu Memorial Trophy game, and I happened to be the lone reporter at the ground. In those simpler times and at such low-profile matches, there were no press boxes. The players sat on plastic chairs outside the dinky pavilion at the ground and the spectators, the few that turned up, were in makeshift stands only metres away.

What enabled our first interaction was the quirky fact that we smoked the same brand of cigarette. One of us—I can't remember who—was either short of a cigarette or of a light. From then on I spent many days sitting next to Vasoo Sir, watching cricket. It was an immersive experience—at once an education in the nuances of cricket and an opportunity to watch the game through the eyes of someone who always thought like a captain and was always a few steps ahead of the scoreboard.

Vasoo Sir was an established player and coach, a legend around the traps. That a man of his calibre should give his time and wisdom so freely to someone wetting his beak in journalism and cricket was unimaginable for me at the time.

This is the kind of generosity that nobody expects. And for someone who was basically an empty vessel, every opportunity to fill up, to drink from the fountain of knowledge directly was a life-changing experience.

But I am far from alone in this. As you will see in the pages that follow, there isn't one person who has had the fortune of meeting Vasoo Sir and who hasn't had his life changed immeasurably for the better by that encounter. In the course of putting together this book, while seeking out people, I met players, from across generations, who have been the backbone of Indian cricket and who have been influenced by Vasoo Sir.

Sunil Gavaskar often recalls with typical pride the manner in which Vasoo instilled in him respect for the game, for team spirit, as well as an affinity for the culture of cricket. If it had not been for Vasoo Sir, the world would not have known one of the greatest cricketers of all time by the name Sunny, which has stuck with him for life.

W.V. Raman, another former cricketer and now a coach with whom I have had the good fortune of spending considerable time, is also a raconteur of the Vasoo Paranjape school of storytelling. In his essay, 'The Coach I would Reach Out To', Raman recalls with great affection his interactions with Vasoo Sir over the years, starting with when he was a player to the time when their bond blossomed into friendship.

But it isn't only the stars of yesteryear who hold Vasoo Sir in reverence. Rohit Sharma, who is at the peak of his powers as a cricketer, a modern classic if you will, readily sat down to have coffee with us and talk about Vasoo Sir. His thoughts have been compiled in the form of an essay that appears in this book under the title 'A Father Figure'. It was Vasoo Sir who got Rohit his first big break. After watching Rohit bat at Wankhede during a practice session at a Mumbai Under-17 camp, Vasoo went straight to the captain, Prashant Naik, and told him that Rohit simply must be included in the playing eleven for one of their practice matches. Rohit recalls the effect Vasoo had on him and how that influence has stayed with him for life: 'He treated all of us like his own children, not as cricketers. We never felt that we were training under a coach. He was more like a father figure to us.'

Then there is Yuvraj Singh, a happy-go-lucky cricketer on the outside but a sensitive and vulnerable person on the inside—something you only get to see when he opens up. And that takes some doing. Yuvraj, whose career I had the good fortune of following, from its under-19 days to its eventual conclusion in June 2019, was as frank when speaking about Vasoo Sir as he was fearless at the crease. 'I was very young when I first met Vasoo Sir and had never met a coach like him . . . He made me feel so comfortable, I still don't know how he did it . . . He had a way of disarming you, making you feel like you had known him all your life . . .'

Yuvraj is someone who has an intense aversion to talking about technique, although he worked on the technical aspect of his game just as hard as anyone else who played on that level. In 'Learning to Love the Game', Yuvraj tells us, 'When you were batting in the nets and Vasoo was watching you, he would say the simplest things: "Watch the ball, Yuvi"; "Wait for it, Yuvi"; "Don't try to hit it so hard, Yuvi". Only later did I realize that he was making technical adjustments to my game without me knowing it.'

The most emotional of all interactions in the course of working on this project was the one with Ramesh Powar. Vasoo Paranjape helped Powar take charge of his life at a time when the latter was about to give up on the game—he had lost a parent and was in dire financial straits. Remembering those times, Powar had to, more than once, put down his cup of coffee, trying to hold back tears. Eventually he couldn't control it. The waiting staff at the Bandra Kurla Complex coffee shop looked daggers at me as Powar, a grown man, broke down and wept freely, burying his head in his hands.

'Vasoo Sir was the one who helped change the way people looked at me,' Powar tells us in 'The Man Who Changed My Life'. 'While I thought I was a nobody, Vasoo Sir had faith in me. I won't call him my guru, because a guru is someone who just teaches you. To me, he is much more than that: a guiding light that appeared in my life at the right time. Without him I would have been nowhere.'

From emotional to cerebral, from deep and profound to light and frothy, there was a new Vasoo story around every corner and with everyone I approached. Ajay Jadeja recalled how, at an under-17 camp he attended in Srinagar, a batsman from Karnataka made more runs than most others. He also bowled a bit of leg spin, but given how unorthodox he was and how little he turned the ball, nobody took much notice of his bowling. But, of course, Vasoo Sir did. He predicted back then that it was with the ball that this boy from Karnataka would make his mark. The boy's name: Anil Kumble, who became India's highest wicket-taker and one of the greatest bowlers ever.

Meeting Kumble in his office in Bangalore offered a new insight into his life and into his relationship with Vasoo Paranjape. Kumble, who is plain-speaking and blunt but never discourteous, showed a much softer side of his personality. 'He spoke to me first about the basics of spin bowling,' Kumble says about Vasoo Sir in 'Time for a Chat'. 'Simple things like how to cock your wrist, how to time your jump in your run-up, when to pause . . . And I wrote all of these things down on the back page of a diary I carried with me at the time. I wish I had that diary today.' This book includes a priceless document from Kumble's past: a letter he wrote to Vasoo as a seventeen-year-old. But I won't speak of it here. Rather, you should read it for yourself to discover what a young cricketer trying to find his place in the world had to say to a coach who became more than a guide to him.

To round things off, I will leave you with the thoughts of another legend from Bangalore who has moved on to coaching. Rahul Dravid is intensely guarded when speaking about anything. I have not come across a cricketer more conscious of his image or of the words he uses—not in a negative way, but in a way that is sometimes frustrating for a journalist in pursuit of an interesting line. And yet, when it came to speaking about Vasoo Sir, Dravid let his guard down completely and spoke from the heart. 'He was truly, deeply in love with the game,' Dravid tells us in 'The Empathetic Coach'. 'He inspired me first as a cricketer and inspires me now in my coaching career.'

There's much more in these pages. I can only say that it has been a journey of extraordinary privilege for me—putting the book together and speaking to the best in the game about a man who is widely regarded as one of a kind. Vasoo Sir is not just a cricket coach. He is not just a friend, philosopher and guide to so many cricketers. He is an institution. His legacy will live on forever, even if he laughs it off with a joke, a shrug and a warm embrace.

Anand Vasu

Falling in Love with Cricket

Jatin Paranjape

Cross Maidan in Mumbai has eight pitches, each leased out to a different cricket club. The two most competitive clubs, National Cricket Club and Karnataka Sports Club, are based at opposite ends of this ground.

It was a Sunday afternoon in November sometime in the late '70s. The Karnataka Sports Club was hosting the Dadar Union Sporting Club for a Police Shield match. The format was interesting: 70 overs a side in a game that would last a day and a half, scheduled to begin at 1 p.m. on Saturday and to conclude at 10 a.m. on Sunday. The 70-over format was a test of one's skills. There was nowhere to hide in this format. You couldn't play it safe by aiming for a draw. You either won or lost.

On that day, Dadar Union was expected to win. But Sharad Rao and Suresh Shetty of the KSC had them on their knees. DU's formidable batting line-up was back in the tent. And things were quiet in the DU tent. Silence in a cricket dressing room is not a good sign. Silence means tension.

It means apprehension. It means a sense of impending doom, a sense that something bad would befall the team.

Dadar Union was in deep trouble. Their captain, his best days as a batsman behind him, was at the crease. He was in the team because he was their best leader, someone whom people looked up to and followed blindly. He expected his team to match the high standards he'd himself set in the past. His troops knew that. They also knew that he could pull them out of this situation. They knew he could still bat. These were the late '70s. No helmets. Creams, not whites. Handshakes after wickets and victories, not wild celebrations. Those were the days of gentlemanly behaviour in the gentleman's game.

Fast bowlers are at their best when they have a couple of wickets under their belt. Young fast bowlers are at their best when they see an ageing ex-professional on strike. Invariably, a few bouncers were meted out to this batsman. One bouncer ricocheted off the top edge of his bat and struck him square on the mouth. There was a loud smack heard as far back as the tent! The umpires ran towards the batsman. The fielders ran towards him. His creams had been bloodied instantaneously. The Dadar Union players rushed out to the middle, but the batsman sent them back with a wave of his hand. He declined even a glass of water out of the aluminum kettle. Thanking the umpires and the fielders, he took guard once again. The bowler bounced him again, and there was another smack. But this time it was the sound of the willow making contact with leather. Six! A furious counter-attack followed. The opposition was taken by surprise.

Even as I excitedly recorded each boundary and run in the scorebook—I was keeping score—I felt deeply worried for that veteran skipper manning the fort: my father, Vasoo Paranjape. His bleeding hadn't stopped. Three of his teeth had been knocked out of his mouth . . . But the match was won! That's all that mattered to him.

He handed over the kitbag to me, and we drove home as if nothing had happened. As if he hadn't just won a tough match. As if he hadn't lost three of his teeth. As if his precious creams hadn't been bloodied . . . We just drove home. And then, a phone call was made to the doctor. My father had to be given stitches. I was asked to get two bottles of Thums Up for him, as he wasn't allowed to eat for some time. The family sat around him silently as he sipped the cold beverage . . .

That was the day I fell in love with Dadar Union and with cricket! That day onwards, cricket became much more than a game for me. It became clear to me that this sport wasn't about individuals; it was about the team. It was about the partnership of eleven individuals galvanized by a sense of common belief and unified by a captain who makes them believe in themselves

I started looking forward to everything cricket. I was taking my early steps into the sport at that time and was equally thrilled about my role as the scorekeeper at Dadar Union's weekend matches. I was the quiet attendee at their Thursday evening team meetings at our house, held over cups of tea made by my mother. I would listen to their planning very carefully. Every scenario was planned, down to a T! Today's video analysts, with all the software tools at their disposal, would have been much better off if they could match up to that level of thinking. The team was mostly young, with a few old soldiers—like V.S. Patil, Suresh Tigdi, Urmikant Modi and my father—in their ranks. The others were Young Turks waiting to make the world their own. They just listened while their seniors spoke. They just executed the plan on the field. They just believed in Vasoo Paranjape.

Despite his age, my father was one of the most brilliant fielders in Mumbai cricket. I think this went a long way in bolstering the team's admiration for him. In that game against the KSC, the loudest gasp and cheer was made for a catch taken by Vasoo, the skipper, at backward short leg. Yes, those were the days of the backward short leg, positioned square of the batsman, at a distance near enough for the ball to carry and far enough for the fielder to be out of harm's way.

Sanjay Manjrekar led Dadar Union for many years. He was an astute captain, a terrific player, and he was one of my early heroes along with Jitendra ('Jitu') Thakre. Having learned under my father as a Dadar Union Young Turk, Sanjay went on to become a pro and played for India.

One season, in their last Kanga League match against Indian Gymkhana, Dadar Union was faced with a tricky situation. They needed a win to claim the Kanga League. Sanjay called for a quick huddle. I was playing for DU by this time.

'We will go for 5 points,' he told us. 'Doesn't matter if we lose outright, but we will go for 5 points to try and win the League.' That was it. Sanjay is a direct guy. What you see is what you get. In many ways he is the last flagbearer of the Dadar Union forthrightness.

We won the toss, put them in to bat and rolled them over. But we were in trouble when it was our turn to bat. Indian Gymkhana had two young fast bowlers from R.A. Podar College: Anil Vazirani and Shashi Krishnan. But we kept attacking. We were down to number eleven, but Sanjay's instructions did not change. We kept attacking. Ajit Puthran hit a huge six over extra cover off Shashi Krishnan, and we were home. No wild cheering. Just handshakes and well-dones. And we went back home. Those were the days. Team above self. Game above self. Teamwork beyond personal goals.

My father was watching that game. As was V.S. Patil. But not once did they come up and get in Sanjay's way. They believed in Sanjay. They believed that the captain would make the right decisions and that the players would show the right intent. I was greatly influenced by all this happening around me. I became a fan of each team member but always kept that fandom to myself. I wanted to prove that I could do it on the pitch along with the rest of the guys.

My father gave me that opportunity. There was no fast-tracking of any kind, never. I had to put in the hard yards, playing down the order. And when an opportunity presented itself, one of the senior batsmen being unavailable, I was told in the dressing room, 'Jatin, you're batting three today. Play freely.'

'Play freely.' I heard this phrase for the first time that day, and I used it throughout my career as a player and a captain. Whenever I was tense at the crease, that voice came back to me: 'Play freely, Jatin.'

I batted number three for my school and college, and only those who bat three know of the pride associated with that number. When I debuted for Mumbai, I was praying that I be sent in to bat at my number. Even if that were to be the only game I ever played for Mumbai, I wanted to bat at my number. Number three. It's a beautiful zone within the beautiful game. At number three you have to be versatile. You can go in at 0 for 1 or at 200 for 1. Being number three is like being a midfielder in football. You have to set the stage for the poster boys of four, five and six. You have to gut it out. Number threes are battlers; they are battle-scarred. They are also the fulcrum of the batting line-up. (I was a left-hander, and being a left-hander at three is an added advantage. The angles change; the bowlers struggle with their lines.)

My attachment to number three was another product of my father's tutelage. He'd once asked Jitu Thakre to bat at three so that Sanjay Manjrekar could go in at four. It was troop formation at its best. Jitu was aggressive. He took the bowlers on and gave Sanjay some cushion at four. I was sold on the idea. Thereafter, all I wanted to do was to play for Mumbai at number three.

As a kid keeping score for Dadar Union, I was witness to their most intricate playing strategies. Bringing the field up and attacking when the well-set batsmen at the crease expected Dadar Union to defend was a common ploy— one that the most experienced batsmen fell for. The use of left-arm spin as the linchpin of the bowling attack was also something I learned at Dadar Union. I learnt the importance of keeping your main bowlers fresh, so that they can make good use of the breeze and the tide (Mumbai being a port city, the ball swings here after teatime as the tide comes in). I learnt how to change batting order game by game, as the situation demanded, without demotivating the batsmen.

My father was brilliant at all of this. He once said to me, 'Jatin, somebody in your team wants it more than the others on any given day. A leader's job is to know who that guy is.'

More than of his cricketing talent, I am an admirer of my father's giving nature. He has helped so many cricketers—hundreds of them—with his advice and encouragement. This memoir is an attempt to spread the word on that aspect of his life and to celebrate the art of giving in cricket.

On and Off the Field

Lalita Paranjape

'Passion' is a word frequently bandied about these days and often used loosely. Many people claim to be 'passionate' about many things. An honourable exception to this passionate stereotype is my husband, Vasoo, who is intensely passionate about cricket in every way.

As an old friend, now departed, eulogized him in a postcard, 'Vasoo, in love with cricket in all its glory, outstanding coach and student of the game . . . somewhere behind the nets even today . . . long live his romance for the game.' The postcard bears this name and address: 'To, Vasoo Paranjape, Somewhere in Hindu Colony, thinking and talking Cricket and Music.' Believe me, this postcard from the UK was delivered to our home!

Vasoo is a maverick in every sense of the word. He does not behave and think like everyone else but has independent and unusual opinions. He does not always conform to established views, choosing to live life on his own terms.

His opinions are remarkably original. And as a cricketing thinker, he has been far ahead of his time.

I am tempted to quote Sir Don Bradman. 'I set great store in certain qualities, which I believe to be essential in addition to skill,' he once said. 'They are that the person conducts his or her life with dignity, with integrity, courage, and perhaps, most of all, with modesty.' I like to believe that these words have influenced Vasoo deeply.

As Vasoo says, 'The two Gods in my small world are Sir Don Bradman and our own Bharat Ratna Shrimati Lata Mangeshkar.' Throughout his career Vasoo endeavoured to emulate the values laid down by Sir Don, and I feel he succeeded in this to a great extent.

Vasoo and I got married in 1962 while I was still in college. We were both very young: he was twenty-four and I was eighteen. I was not even remotely interested in sports and had no idea about cricket. Vasoo's sister, Suhasini, was married to my brother Shashikant, and Vasoo and I got to know each other during their wedding. We were instantly drawn to each other, and we decided to get married a year later.

We now have three children—Dr Radhika Shah, Dr Shubhada Jagasia and Jatin—and six grandchildren. Both my daughters are doctors and so are my sons-in-law. My daughter-in-law, Gandhali, has been a journalist and now helps Jatin in running their sports start-up, Khelo More. Jatin followed in his father's footsteps, playing cricket competently right from school through college, then getting selected for Mumbai in the Ranji Trophy tournament, playing for India A in Pakistan and eventually representing the national team.

While Vasoo pursued cricket, I entered academics and taught courses on English language and English literature at Ramnarain Ruia College in Matunga, Mumbai.

We have been married for close to fifty-five years and have had a reasonably stable and fulfilling relationship. We have had our share of ups and downs too, like everyone else, but we have managed to navigate pretty smoothly through life. Things were not easy for me initially as I did not have a sports background, and I had difficulty adjusting to Vasoo's demanding cricket routine. He was never home on weekends and had little time for the family. But as time passed, I began to understand that he was at the peak of his career and needed my support.

Vasoo never stopped me from fulfilling my academic pursuits. Both he and my mother-in-law, Leelabai Paranjape, a very respected and cultured lady, supported me wholeheartedly and encouraged me to complete my graduation and post-graduation.

Probably, Vasoo was the more understanding partner every time I was short-tempered and petulant during the early years of our marriage, when I was coping with home, kids, my own studies, my career and trying to adapt to a different lifestyle. Over the years, our relationship has evolved and stabilized, and as I look back, I feel that mutual respect and trust have been the hallmarks of our partnership.

I want to share some of Vasoo's personal traits with readers.

At the top of the list is his deep reverence for this great game. For him, cricket is a religion; it towers above everything else. It is not just a game; it's a sacred commitment and a way of life for him.

A strong sense of fair play is deeply ingrained in his character. His credo is: play the game according to the rules; when the umpire's finger goes up, bow your head and walk back. He firmly believes that to play well and to succeed, you need character and grit. And he believes that your character is reflected in the way you play.

If it is to be enjoyed, cricket has to be played in the right spirit. And the game has to be enjoyed; 'winning at any cost' is not his philosophy.

For Vasoo, cricket is a team sport above all. If you play only for yourself, you are doing a disservice to your team. If you are leading your side, you ought to take all your players along with you and lead by example, from the front. You ought to enable your team to accept the challenges the game poses to them. You ought to enable them to take risks and to play to their full potential.

Vasoo is an excellent reader of the game because he watches cricket closely and minutely, always drawing on his own vast experience as a cricketer. (It's worth mentioning here that he has won more than fifty-five championships in five different tournaments in club cricket.) An avid reader, almost exclusively of books about cricket, Vasoo has a large collection of reading material—books as well as articles preserved in the shape of newspaper and magazine clippings—on the subject. He has been a lifelong admirer of great cricket writers, such as Jack Fingleton and Neville Cardus.

His club Dadar Union instilled in him the value of discipline. As a cricketer, he was always meticulous about his sporting attire—his shoes and laces were always clean; his pads neatly strapped and polished; his bat well-oiled; and his trademark scarf spotless.

Vasoo's sense of humour, too, is legendary. Countless stories of his wit and repartee have gone viral on social media and are endlessly recounted whenever cricketers meet. Some of these have already been mentioned elsewhere in the book, so I will not repeat them. People love him for his clean and spontaneous sense of humour, which is never malicious or sarcastic. He is a humorist and not a satirist. On innumerable occasions, his humorous interventions have defused tough situations by taking the pressure off the players.

When our children were growing up, an unwritten rule was that all of us had to have dinner together and talk about how we spent the day. Curfew time was 7.30 p.m. The children were around us at team meetings and followed the discussions closely. Vasoo always had a way with children. During the summer, Vasoo's sisters would spend time with us in Matunga with their kids, and he spent many happy evenings with his nieces and nephews sitting on the large teakwood swing on our terrace. A much-awaited summer event was the churning of mango ice cream on the hand-operated ice-cream maker, with all the kids taking turns at it. My nieces and nephews—grown-ups now—are still nostalgic about the happy summers they spent in their grandma's and Bal Mama Mami's home (Vasoo is called Bal in the family).

Punctuality is the hallmark of a cricketer. Vasoo always reached the ground much ahead of the other players, and woe to him who sauntered in late (the latecomer was promptly dropped and asked to do the scorekeeping). Consequently, my children and I, too, learnt the importance of punctuality.

A great quality of Vasoo's is his ability to motivate people and get the best out of them. He is always respectful towards everyone, be they high or low. He was never envious of any player. His honesty and integrity earned him respect in the world of cricket, and he always held his head high. Never one to be cowed by others into doing or saying something, Vasoo held fast to his opinions even in the face of opposition and could persuade his detractors to change their minds.

In life as in cricket, he always played with a straight bat. And he preferred to be away from the limelight. 'My job,' he once said, 'is on the cricket field.' He shunned publicity, never hankered after accolades, never applied for government awards. ('How can you apply for a state award? I will never do that.') Despite having played in the Ranji Trophy for Bombay for ten years, he never once signed up for a benefit match. 'Cricket has given me everything. I am content,' was what Vasoo, who never chased Mammon and has never been interested in monetary gains, would say. Generous to a fault, he has helped many cricketers in their careers.

To his children, he is a good father—someone who taught them sportsmanship; taught them that life, like sports, has its ups and downs and must be faced with equanimity. To be sure, his honesty and integrity have influenced them deeply.

They have learned from him that they must give the benefit of the doubt to the other person and not criticize them. Because of Vasoo, there is team spirit in the family too!

His advice to his children is to keep life simple and be happy. A believer in the philosophy of the Bhagavad Gita, he has a stoical, balanced approach to life, neither swayed too much by joy nor by sorrow. We celebrate Ganesh Chaturthi and Navratri at our place; these are our annual rituals. And he recites the Ganpati *stotra* and Maruti *stotra* every day.

Vasoo is a born raconteur. Back in the day, he was always surrounded by his teammates, by players from rival clubs and by his fans. They flocked to him, and he regaled them with his cricket stories, which were laced with his witticisms and jokes that would have them in splits! On Sundays, if there was a match at the neighbouring ground, his team would come for a quick curd-rice lunch, to be washed down with fresh buttermilk.

A friend once said, 'I don't know how Lalita manages to cook for eleven people. At her place, guests are always in multiples of eleven!' Looking back, I don't know how I managed, though sometimes I would throw up my hands in despair, wishing I had Draupadi's inexhaustible vessel, the Akshay Patra. The best part was that we all enjoyed having guests over, and our bonds with them grew very strong. Even unannounced visitors were welcome, and we still keep an open house. Vasoo is the true *ajatshatru*—a man without enemies, a good friend to all, loved by all!

My Tryst with Cricket

Vasoo Paranjape

My tryst with cricket began way back in the 1940s. I lived in a typical Maharashtrian Brahmin joint family, in a sprawling ancestral house located in the leafy suburb of Matunga, Mumbai. Along with my parents and two sisters, there was an assortment of aunts, uncles and lots of cousins, all under one roof at Ganesh Bhuvan, the house my grandfather, Ganesh Narayan Paranjape, built and named after himself.

Two of my aunts came from cricket-loving families in Pune. My elder aunt's brother, a diehard cricket fan, lived with us as he was working in Mumbai at the time. He was the one who regaled me with cricketing anecdotes, and he took me to watch local cricket matches and sometimes even to the big matches at the Brabourne Stadium. He spoke about well-known cricketers, like D.B. Deodhar, S.G. Shinde, S.W. Sohoni, Khandu Rangnekar and Dattu Phadkar (who was then the poster boy of Indian cricket).

By that time I had started playing for my school and my interest in the game had increased. I must have been ten or twelve years old when I watched Denis Compton and Vinoo Mankad playing at the Cricket Club of India in a Ranji final.

By 1947–48, I was training at the New Hind Club nets and became a member of the Dadar Union Sporting Club at Matunga. I was given a two-year playing membership by the P.J. Hindu Gymkhana in Mumbai. I was a left-arm slow-spin bowler, and I used to bowl the chinaman as a regular part of my armoury.

It was a big occasion for me when, one day, I saw all the Indian players playing at the adjoining Matunga Gymkhana ground, including the great Vijay Merchant. Watching me bowl, Merchant called me over for a chat. However, I was so awestruck that I couldn't muster the courage to respond. In retrospect, my love for the game of cricket originated with that encounter!

I studied at the King George School and was the captain of the junior team there. When King George played in the Harris Shield tournament for the first time ever, I was leading the team. And I led the team through our first-ever attempt at the Giles Shield tournament as well—we became champions that very year. I was lucky to be selected as skipper for the Giles Shield after my miserable debut in the Harris Shield. (Playing at number eleven, I was run out for nought in the Vinoo Mankad style—the bowler taking off the bails at the runner's end before delivering the ball—despite the numerous warnings from the captain and senior players that this might happen to me!)

During this period, I had the advantage of being coached by the great Homi Vajifdar, who was the first Bombay captain. Vajifdar was a big man with powerful wrists. He was an all-rounder and a great slip fielder, and he played for Parsee Gymkhana. He was the coach at the Tairsee nets conducted by the P.J. Hindu Gymkhana. Leading by example, Vajifdar taught us the value of being a good person. He was disciplined, meticulous and had an eye for detail. If you trained with him, your shoes had to be properly polished and your cricket attire had to be perfect. He always said, 'Whatever you do, you must be the best at it.' Though he was not imposing in any way, he commanded respect. He had a liberal, democratic approach to the game and gave everyone a chance. He instilled in us the idea of fair play and taught us the meaning of sportsmanship. The Tairsee wicket was so immaculately prepared and maintained under his supervision that some of the older players always wanted to go and play there to get back in form. My cricketing future took shape under this great man, and my career progressed in the right direction. I was lucky to have him as a coach in my formative years.

Since I was made an honorary playing member of the P.J. Hindu Gymkhana, I represented them in local matches. I recollect having once taken 4 wickets in 4 balls in a Purshottam Shield match. This feat had been previously achieved only by Dattu Phadkar, and I had equalled it.

Then, Vinoo Mankad became the coach at the P.J. Hindu Gymkhana. And some time later, I was given the privilege of becoming the head coach at the Tairsee nets. That was a proud moment for me. This progression, from 1953, led me to Dadar Union, with which my association has continued till today and will continue for as long as I live.

It took me some time to get into the Dadar Union playing eleven, mainly because they were such a strong team. Playing under Madhav Mantri and with Ramnath Kenny, the Amladi brothers, Naren Tamhane and P.K. Kamat was a lifetime's cricketing experience. We played the Kanga League, the Talim Shield, the Purshottam Shield, the Comrade Shield. And we built an outstanding record. I wonder if any other team has won the Comrade Shield, the Purshottam Shield and the Talim Shield as many times as we did.

No account of Dadar Union can be complete without a mention of the bowling duo of V.S. 'Marshall' Patil and Urmikant Mody. Hardly a match passed without them giving us an early breakthrough.

My time at Dadar Union taught me just what a club can mean to a player and what a player should mean to a club. When I watched how Dadar Union went about things and compared that with how some of the other clubs went about their business, it became amply clear to me that I was fortunate to be a part of this great institution. I am not criticizing other clubs, but for me Dadar Union was the right club. And I fit in at the club. It is the sense of belonging it evokes that makes a club great.

As a captain, I was always conscious of the responsibility I had to each and every player of Dadar Union. Having come up through the ranks myself in a club that had a proud tradition and put a strong accent on success, I knew what a youngster trying to get in and make his mark would feel like. I knew when someone needed an arm around the shoulder or just a quiet word. After all, the captain's role is not limited to calling heads or tails at the toss and setting the field. The captain must always remember that while he is leading his men, he is also representing his club. I spent a lifetime imbibing the Dadar Union ethos. What good would it have been had I not passed it on to the generations that came after?

Dadar Union's Glory Days[*]

Dadar Union Sporting club was a formidable force in Mumbai cricket, with some of the greatest players in Indian cricketing history—exceptional batsmen, bowlers and fielders all—associated with it. And for many decades, the team was led by an equally exceptional captain, Vasoo Paranjape.

He was part of Dadar Union's Kanga League-winning team on twelve occasions. This is Paranjape's past, his distant past. But his memories of that time are plentiful. Here's what he told us about his Kanga League-playing days.

The early years

'I joined Dadar Union in 1953, when Madhav Mantri was captain. We never had any meetings but focused on fielding

---

[*] Excerpts from an interview with Vasoo Paranjape, by Clayton Murzello. First published in the *Sunday Mid-May* on 4 September 2004. What appears here is an edited version of the original.

a month before the league. Mantri used to come from work at 6.05 p.m., remove his tie, get into his cricket attire, and we practised like maniacs.'

Discipline was king

'Discipline was top-class. Once, before going out for the toss, Mantri told Ramnath Kenny, who had just arrived at the stadium, that he was not in the team because he was late. Now, Kenny had just played for India against Australia in 1959–60, but there was no compromise as far as discipline was concerned.'

Driving them around

'I would pick up Dilip [Vengsarkar] and Sunny [Gavaskar], and we would go for the matches. Sunny used to call me whenever he returned from England to say that he would be playing with us. Sunny never got a Kanga League hundred for us. But then we did not bat long in this bowler-friendly league, and the totals rarely crossed the 100 mark.'

What made us a force

'A family atmosphere. Terrific bowlers, terrific batsmen and even more terrific fielders. We were a great fielding unit. Daya Dudhwadkar, Suresh Tigdi, Avinash Karnik, Ramnath Parkar, with Sunny in the slips and myself.'

'V' for victory

'Vithal Patil was a great bowler. Uniquely—and Sunny will agree with me—his appeals were almost never declined. When that happened, he would just look at me, say sorry to the umpire and get back to his mark. I would say 97 per cent of his appeals were given out. He used to bowl stump-to-stump and very accurate. Urmikant Mody devastated batting attacks from the other end.'

Dilip Sardesai spoke too early

'At one point in the early 1970s, we did not have the services of V.S.Patil, who was unwell. We were playing against the Cricket Club of India at the Brabourne Stadium and were all out for 64. Their side included Sunny, Milind Rege, Polly Umrigar, Bapu Nadkarni, G.S. Ramchand, Hanumant Singh, Mahesh Sampat, Karsan Ghavri, and K.S. Indrajitsinhji. I was sitting in the pavilion during the lunch break when the radio commentator Anand Setalvad asked me, "Do you have any chances now?" I said, "You might win but you will be on your knees before you do that." Dilip Sardesai was on the phone telling someone that he would be late since the CCI were trying to earn an innings victory. They reached 34 for 1, but Jitendra Bhutta claimed 4 wickets in an over, and the CCI were bowled out for 42. That match gave me immense satisfaction.'

Going for the win

'Dadar Union were playing against the Rajasthan Sports Club in a Police Shield match, if I am not mistaken. The format was a day and a half, and we were playing at the New Hind stadium at Matunga Maidan. New Hind had short boundaries, so big totals could be chased down fairly easily there.

'We scored 275 or so, and at lunch on the second day Rajasthan were in a good position, with both Vijay Alva and Lalchand Rajput playing well. Madhav Mantri, a Dadar Union senior, dropped in to watch the game, and during lunchtime we had an animated conversation about captaincy. We talked about our distinct approaches to it: his defensive way of leading a team, and my attacking way, which was aimed at winning the game and allowed for a risk or two. When the umpires walked out to the middle, I got up from the chair and said, "If Rajasthan are 200 for no loss at tea, you will see that only attacking cricket will win the game for us."

'And lo and behold, soon Rajasthan were 200 for no loss, with Alva and Rajput batting on 100 each. In the post-tea session, I threw the ball to Suru Nayak, who was an accurate leg-spinner, and I told him, "Suru, let's pull the field in and attack both the batsmen for the next fifteen minutes. They won't be expecting it. The ball is turning, and there's risk involved if they go for the big shots. You either make this game for me or break this game."

'The first over after tea. Suru bowled a tossed-up leg spin on middle stump, and Rajput went inside out and holed out to me at mid-off. We had opened a small window of hope. Suru then bowled brilliantly and ran through Rajasthan. Dadar Union won yet another game, staying true to our strength, which was to play attacking cricket and force a win.'

Achrekar was a class act

'Test players apart, I would rate Ramakant Achrekar as the best Kanga League batsman I saw. His defensive play was immaculate, and he could read the swing of the ball well.'

The Mantri masterclass

'What I learnt form Madhav Mantri most of all were his field placements. His immediate juniors felt that he was a great captain. Subhash Gupte and Vijay Manjrekar always said that India would have done very well on its 1959 tour to England had Mantri been the captain.'

Dadar Union's decline

'Fortunes rise and fall. It's the course of nature. You don't find dedicated people at Dadar Union anymore. You drop a player for two matches and he's off to another club. I used to get dropped at Dadar Union because I was the eighth Ranji Trophy player in the side. The Talim Shield had a ridiculous rule that only seven Ranji players could play in one team.'

Where's the class?

'We won the Ranji Trophy two years in a row. But how many players have we given to the national team? Class has gone down, replaced by mass culture. An increase in the number of shorter-format games has also led to cricketers having to make a decision on which formats to focus on and sadly, commerce dictates that they focus more on white-ball cricket rather than on red-ball cricket. The IPL has certainly increased the pool of professional cricketers manifold but it has come at a heavy cost: it has changed the cricketing culture and the mindset of youngsters, who don't think much about why they are playing the game in the first place. This actually places a lot more responsibility on the BCCI and on our state cricket associations to think hard about the structure and tiering of domestic tournaments like the Ranji Trophy. State associations also need to find new ways to support junior and club cricket within their purview. The custodians of this great game have a lot to think about and their role has never been more important than now.'

In the Footsteps of Don and Beyond: On Sunil Gavaskar

Vasoo Paranjape

When I saw him for the first time, Sunny was a young boy who would accompany his father to Dadar Union games. Right from that time I could sense how serious he was about batting. He would play on the sidelines, with one of the team members chucking balls at him endlessly. He played with a very straight bat—quite uncommon for a beginner, as your instinct is to put power into the shot with your bottom hand, which then changes the angle of your bat from the vertical to the horizontal.

I could see his hunger to learn and his commitment to practice from the very start, and I was extremely keen on bringing him into the Dadar Union team as soon as possible. After he joined the squad, he took to his team members very easily, and they to him. Sunny was a team man to the core, and it hurt him when Dadar Union lost a match. He made an impact as a Dadar Union batsman very early on and soon made a name for himself in Mumbai's cricketing circles, along with Milind Rege, his best friend, who was a wonderful all-rounder and whom I rated very highly.

Sunny was also a very good close-in fielder, and I drilled into him the importance of being a good all-round fielder too. He was always attentive and respectful.

I also stressed that he should field in the slips, to improve his concentration while batting. Undoubtedly, playing for Dadar Union enabled him to enter this great game through the most challenging route, and I feel that this beginning helped him immensely throughout his career.

Little did I realize the enormity of the task ahead of me when I consented to write an article on Sunny. So much has been written, and will be written, about him in various magazines that to cover his record-breaking career in one solitary article is itself tantamount to a record-setting feat.

When the Australians arrived in London way back in 1930, Bill Woodfull, the Australian captain, while presenting his team introduced Don Bradman as the holder of more records than a gramophone company! This description fits Sunny more than any of his contemporaries. His records—the centuries, the batting aggregate and the century partnerships—remain landmarks in international cricket.

It was early in his cricketing life that Sunny developed an appetite for the game and an ability to stay in the middle for a long innings. He continued to consistently grow as a player through school, college, varsity, club and early Ranji Trophy matches. By the beginning of the '70s, he looked the very picture of a top-class opening batsman, as if made to order.

His deserving and timely selection into the Indian squad that toured the West Indies in 1971 paved the way for his unforgettable debut performance. He played his first international match in the second Test of the series, and it was Sunny's praiseworthy batting in that game that led to the first-ever Indian victory on West Indian soil.

This blazed a glittering trail of brilliant performances by him on that tour, with a century and a double-century in the last Test in Trinidad. He scored 774 runs in the series: a debut performance that remains unmatched.

Subsequently, during the 1971–72 season, I watched him play for the Rest of the World team in Australia, and that was the only occasion that I saw him a little perturbed by the bounce rather than the pace of the Australian wickets. On his following visits Down Under, he overcame this anxiety through insightful and intelligent thinking. He started positioning himself more beside the ball than behind it. He did not, however, have a very convincing series against Dennis Lillee's men on his last tour of Australia in 1980–81. A missed opportunity that probably nags him still.

On all his English tours, though, he invariably excelled. He had an intuitive ability to adjust to the varying conditions of the English atmosphere and pitches. The matchless 221 he scored at the Oval, during the 1979–80 season, in challenging conditions was possibly the pinnacle of his career, though the 101 he made at Old Trafford in typical English conditions probably gave him greater satisfaction. But for all his successes in England, he could never fulfil the ultimate dream that every batsman has—to score a hundred at Lord's, the Mecca of cricket.

For a batsman who played most of his innings in such a strict and disciplined manner, he still couldn't do justice, I believe, to his stroke-making talents. One fully appreciates the responsibilities he carried on his shoulders as an opening batsman—that too in the era of pace bowling—and the captaincy added to his burden.

However, from time to time, he gave us glimpses of his stroking ability, as in the series against the West Indies in 1983. The stroke-studded century he scored in Delhi and the 90 at Ahmedabad must go down as two of the best in his glittering career. After a dubious stroke got him out at Calcutta in the second innings, he promised me he'd do better and asked me to look forward to the Madras Test, where he would make amends for his poor showing in Calcutta. Indeed, his unshakable confidence was on display in Madras; he looked totally invincible in that match.

There were some innings that rightly earned him the wrath of critics. For example, the one he played in the first World Cup (1975); another in the Bangalore Test against England (1981–82); and the above-mentioned innings at Calcutta (1983), to name a few. He himself would not have sat through the video replays of these innings.

It has been remarked that Sunny did not always face the best bowling attacks. For my part, I always believed Sunny could play a convincing innings against any formidable bowling attack. Even if bowlers like Alan Keith Davidson, Dennis Lillee, Imran Khan, Derek Underwood, E.A.S. Prasanna and Subhash Gupte were to be marshalled against him in a play-to-finish match, I would have still bet on Sunny playing better than the other contenders to the title of the world's best batsman.

It would have been a dream come true if this play-to-finish match were to be held at Lord's, with former cricketers given proper seats over the sight screen, and with Sunny walking out to the middle in his perfect 'cricket clothes', in keeping with the highest standards of this great game.

For nearly fifteen years, since his breakthrough tour of Australia in 1977–78, DILIP VENGSARKAR was one of the mainstays of India's Test batting line-up. Tall and slim, he had all the 'touch play' you would expect of someone from the Bombay school of batsmanship. But it was his ability to attack bowlers when the conditions were tough and the situations demanding that set him apart.

While the drive was what Vengsarkar was universally admired for, he also used his height to good effect, cutting and pulling with panache, and this made him dangerous on both front foot and back foot. The Colonel, as Vengsarkar would come to be known, played 116 Tests, scoring centuries all around the world. But he is best known for being the first person to score three Test hundreds against England at sLord's

From his formative years till today, Vengsarkar has been very close to Vasoo Paranjape. Every time you mention the name Paranjape to Vengsarkar, his eyes light up; and the mentor's reaction is much the same when he hears about his mentee. This is a relationship that has strengthened over the years and one that shows no signs of ever becoming any different.

More Than a Mentor

Dilip Vengsarkar

You couldn't miss Vasoo Paranjape. Even if you were a schoolboy cricketer caught up in the challenge of playing the game the right way, like I was in the late '60s, as a junior cricketer for King George School.

Our school team was coached by Vithal Patil, who was Vasoo's valuable teammate at the Dadar Union Sporting Club. To think that all three of us played in the same Dadar Union team from the early 1970s onwards—it seems, at least to me, fairytale-like.

Vasoo was more than a guide at Dadar Union; he was our captain. He was also a man who got excited by talent and endorsed young players before Mumbai's illustrious cricketers. In my case, it was Vinoo Mankad, who watched me getting runs for the club in the 1973 Purshottam Shield final at the P.J. Hindu Gymkhana. Vinoobhai had no hesitation in meeting me after my knock to offer encouraging words. Vasoo had clearly filled Vinoobhai's ears well.

Our captain was always smartly dressed, and you could spot him on the field by his scarf. When you got closer to the action, you could see his astute field placings and smart bowling changes. Vasoo interacted with a lot of stars at Dadar Union, but don't let that lead you to believe that the youngsters and other 'lesser players' were neglected. He ensured his mentoring reached them as well.

Vasoo was quite audible, direct and sharp, but that did not equate to rudeness. When it came to him passing on subtle tips to tighten up a batsman's technique in a solid session, he did so with a dose of humour, and invariably the player would get his point and show improvement. That's how Vasoo did his coaching; that's how he won people over and got the job done. Never have I heard him blow his own trumpet. You got the feeling that Vasoo's only concern was the good of the player.

I am sure he was the one to recommend me to Ajit Wadekar, whose team I was in during our tour to Sri Lanka in 1974. Being in that team of stars helped me immeasurably.

I cherish the days I spent with Vasoo at Dadar Union. We played hard cricket and we had a lot of fun as well, without losing our focus. To say we took our cricket seriously would be an understatement.

We won many a title under Vasoo. I remember he once wanted the team to celebrate with beer after winning a final at the P.J. Hindu Gymkhana. 'Not at Dadar Union,' remarked the stern Vithal 'Marshall' Patil. We could only smile. Vasoo started playing the game in an era different from ours but gelled so well with us. He was like the life of the party, and I am glad he has retained his sense of humour.

SANDEEP PATIL played his cricket in the wrong era. If he were in his prime today, all roads would lead to him. Tall, strapping, handsome, with movie-star looks and a charming personality, Patil was a gifted cricketer as well as an entertainer at the crease. His attacking game made him a crowd-puller, but as a batsman of considerable skill and a canny medium-pacer, his value to the Indian team was indisputable.

He may be best remembered for the 174 he made in Adelaide against an attack that included Dennis Lillee and Len Pascoe—an innings that was very special indeed, as Patil had been struck on the head by a ball delivered by Pascoe in just the previous Test. Equally memorable was his 129 at Old Trafford that included six fours in an over by Bob Willis. But it was his role in India's triumph in the 1983 World Cup that sticks most in memory.

As a cricketer, Patil was shaped by Vasoo Paranjape from a very early age. Even when he was a child, Patil was taken with the image of Paranjape the cricketer, a man who worked magic on the field. And since the time Patil became a Paranjape disciple, the two have shared a close bond, transcending all student-teacher boundaries. To suggest they are family would not be far from the truth.

My Source of Confidence

Sandeep Patil

He was the only one of his kind: our darling coach, Vasoo Sir.

As a school kid, when I watched the Kanga League, there was this smart player from Dadar Union, white cravat round his neck, just like Colonel C.K. Nayudu. He had everything a man could want. He was well-read; he was a great captain, a great fielder and such a great human being. His wit and his timing, these were always with him. Every comment he made—be it at a party or during a drive—sounded historic to us. It was like Shakespeare to our ears.

My first impression of him was that he was very stylish— always well-turned-out, spic and span. Those days, few cricketers paid attention to such things. The white scarf, the cream flannels, the floppy hat . . . Oh, he was a cricketer from head to toe!

And this while leading a side which had Sunil Gavaskar, V.S. Patil, Urmikant Mody, Suresh Tigdi, Dilip Vengsarkar, Amar Vaidya and so many others, against the giants of the

Shivaji Park Gymkhana. It was worth waiting till the end of the match, just to see what he would do, from a captain's strategic perspective. The Kanga League tie between Shivaji Park Gymkhana and Dadar Union was the best; it was our local derby, and I am certain that it was the reason I fell in love with the great game of cricket. My job at these games was only to keep score, but I would still look forward to doing that every year. In those days, we had wooden scoreboards with metal plates for numbers. I had to keep the numbers ticking, and I would get a plate of vada from my father for doing this job, which required me to reach the stadium at 8 a.m. There were thousands of spectators there.

I never thought that I would be playing with him one day or that he would become my coach. It happened so quickly. When I finished school and went to Ramnarain Ruia College, Vasoo Sir was the coach there, and I learned many valuable lessons from him. He taught me the importance of playing positively in any situation and drilled into me the idea that I was a stroke player and that I should follow my natural instincts while playing. We had a very good team at Ruia College, but he made us much better by helping keep our mindsets positive. He laid very strict emphasis on fielding, and we soon became one of the best fielding sides in our circuit. He used to say, 'Fielding is the key to winning, as a half chance if converted can swing the balance of a game.' I loved those years and became a much better player from a game-awareness perspective. I used to captain the team and learned a great deal from him in that department too. He was extremely shrewd and very result-focused, but never did he flout the rules of the game, never tried any gamesmanship with the opposition or with the umpires. In fact, he would always applaud the other team. He was a lover of the game in the truest spirit.

I moved from Ruia College and joined the star-studded Nirlon cricket team, whose manager-cum-coach he was. Here, too, he was my go-to man.

But the real turning point in my life came later, thanks again to Vasoo Sir and Lalita Madam. When I first proposed to my wife Deepa, she refused, twice in a span of six months. Somehow I came to know that Vasoo's and Deepa's fathers were friends. My parents were eager to get me married, and there were other possibilities, but I had decided that I wanted to marry Deepa. Avi Karnik mentioned this to Vasoo, and Vasoo invited Arvind Divekar, Deepa's father, to his place. And you know Vasoo's style. He began by asking him: 'What is your problem? Why is Deepa not giving him a chance?' Then, Vasoo told him, 'Given a chance, even I would get my daughter married to Sandeep, he's such a good boy.' Divekar was immediately convinced. Vasoo later came over and told me: 'Look, I've put in a word for you. Now don't let me down.' Lalita Madam and Vasoo organized a meeting between Deepa and me on the balcony of their Matunga home.

What they did for me changed the course of my life. And I cannot return this favour even in twenty lifetimes. For Vasoo and Lalita Madam, I will do anything.

At Ruia, where Vasoo Sir was our coach, Lalita Madam was our English teacher. On the eve of any match, we would gather on Vasoo Sir's terrace to discuss the strategy for the next day. But for this purpose, we often had to bunk

Lalita Madam's lectures in college. When she arrived at the house, we would hide our faces. But they were both very understanding and both contributed hugely to our lives.

In cricket, a fine line divides confidence from overconfidence. Vasoo, with his lighthearted and funny style of talking, was our source of confidence. My first major match was for West Zone against the touring Australians in Ahmedabad in 1979. Alan Hurst was bowling very fast, and then there was Rodney Hogg. I was extremely nervous yet hell-bent on performing well. It was my BIG chance and all eyes were on me! Before leaving for Ahmedabad I went to meet Vasoo for advice. He said, 'Arré Hurst-worst you burst him.'

In his first over, Hurst bowled a bouncer to our captain Anshuman Gaekwad, who was hit on the head and had to be taken to a hospital. Ghulam Parkar, the other opener, was also hit, and he too was rushed to hospital. I walked out to bat with Vasoo's words ringing in my mind and decided to trust my instincts and attack the Australians. I managed to score 50-odd in that game, thanks to the chat I'd had with Vasoo before the game.

I was then picked for the Indian team, for the 1980–81 Australia tour. They had a terrific pace attack: Dennis Lillee, Jeff Thomson, Rodney Hogg and Len Pascoe. Before boarding the plane, I obviously went back to Vasoo for some advice. This was a huge moment in my cricketing career because as a batsman you dreamt of going to Australia and scoring runs against them. Once again, he boosted my confidence.

He told me in Marathi, in his true style: 'What Dennis Lillee, Lenny Pascoe, Jeff Thomson? You watch them properly for the first fifteen minutes and then let them watch you for the next fifteen months.' And that's almost exactly what happened. I trusted my attacking instincts, and though I was hit on the head by Pascoe, I refused to play defensively. Vasoo's words kept ringing in my mind whenever I felt low on confidence. I scored 174 at Adelaide, and this was one of my most memorable knocks.

Vasoo's advice always touched upon the mental side of the game. It was about strategy. About game-awareness. It made a player focus on the bigger picture and stop stressing about the small things that can break one's concentration. Vasoo was not only a shrewd tactician; he was a very shrewd people manager. He knew how to unify individuals into a team and got them to think positively as a unit.

The stories about his sense of humour are part of the folklore of Indian cricket, and I have lost count of the number of times, as part of the Bombay and Indian cricket teams, I have come across people talking about him and laughing uncontrollably. I want to tell you about the time we were going for a Times Shield match. Vasoo's car was an old Fiat and mine was worse. Some of the players—Karsan Ghavri, Kiran Asher—were in my car and some were in Vasoo's. We were driving up Peddar Road in the rain when Vasoo's car stalled. There was a man driving a taxi right behind Vasoo's car, and he kept honking even as Vasoo was trying to start his car. This went on for ten minutes—we were watching from our car—and then, Vasoo got so bugged he got out of his car, handed over the keys to the taxi driver and told him, 'You please start my car. I'll sit in your car and honk for you.' Only Vasoo can do that!

Playing in schools, maidans, Ranji Trophy leagues and international cricket tournaments, I have encountered many memorable characters, but Vasoo tops the list. He's a treasure from Bombay and remains a darling of the cricketing community here and beyond. From Kapil Dev to Rahul Dravid, from the *paani poori wallah* to the *kaala khatta wallah*—every single person who came across Vasoo can only be grateful to him. That is his beauty. To me he is family, and he taught me the meaning of respect. I need not say more.

'What I Saw in Sandeep . . .'

Sandeep trained under me when I was a coach at Ruia College in Mumbai. He was a free-stroking player. It soon became apparent to me that he had the power and range of shots to turn a match on its head if he batted for the required amount of time. He looked very promising to me right from the get-go. Technique did not matter to him too much; it was more 'see ball, hit ball'. I was mindful that for him to succeed, that simplicity of thought (see ball, hit ball) had to remain with him as the core of his batting.

I remember he scored a brilliant hundred for Bombay in the Ranji Trophy final against Karnataka (1982–83 season). He was batting on zero overnight and scored 121 in a single session (from start of play on the final day till lunchtime). I tried to instil in him the idea that he had to give himself some time at the start of every innings to gauge the pace and bounce of the pitch, as he liked to play the ball on top of the bounce and this involved trusting the pitch, which was only possible once you understood its behaviour, so to speak.

—Vasoo Paranjape

When you think of SACHIN TENDULKAR and coaching, the name that comes to mind is Ramakant Achrekar, the man who is credited with crafting Tendulkar into the player he became. It was Achrekar who handled all things cricket as far as Tendulkar was concerned, taking this unbelievably talented young player under his wing and showing him the value of hard work and discipline. It was indeed Achrekar who sowed the seeds of ambition and sharpened the hunger for runs in Tendulkar—setting a player who might have been very, very good on the path to becoming truly great.

But besides Achrekar, who is justly remembered as Tendulkar's guru, there were a handful of others who played an integral part in the success of one of the greatest batsmen of all time. One of them was Vasoo Paranjape. As Tendulkar reveals in his piece, Paranjape stepped in at just the right times, with an input here and a comment there, a story here and a hug there. Paranjape's role in getting Tendulkar into the thick of things cannot be overestimated, but he never staked a claim on India's crown jewel. Not once has he said, publicly or privately, that he had a role to play in Tendulkar's journey. In fact, when Tendulkar was set to announce his retirement from international cricket, Paranjape was the second person he telephoned. (The first was Achrekar.) 'In an hour, I am going to announce my retirement,' Tendulkar told his beloved Vasoo Sir, who replied with typical candour, 'Thank you for calling, Sachin, but I have not done anything.' Tendulkar's response was telling, 'Sir, I know what you have done for me.'

My Debt to Vasoo Sir

Sachin Tendulkar

'*Yeh lagne wala player nahin, lagaane wala player hai.*'
I am told these are the words that got me my first India call-up. The year was 1989 and India was picking the team to tour Pakistan. I had scored a century at the Irani Trophy, and I was the highest run-getter for Mumbai in the Ranji Trophy that season. Earlier that year, in the month of April, I had been looking forward to getting selected for the West Indies tour. However, the late Raj Singh Dungarpur, fondly known as Raj Bhai to the cricketing world, had told me to focus on my upcoming senior secondary exams, which were just ten days or so away. He had assured me that my selection in the team was not too far in the future and that one day it would definitely happen.

If the selectors had apprehensions about picking me, it would have been understandable. The committee, led by Raj Bhai, may have been worried that it was too early to blood me. Yet, I am told that Raj Bhai made a call to Vasoo Paranjape Sir to enquire about me, and this got me my first break. In his typically clipped voice and witty style, Vasoo Paranjape—Vasoo Sir to me—told Raj Bhai that I was a player who would be dishing it out (*lagaane wala*) to the famous Pakistani fast bowlers and wouldn't be at the receiving end (*lagne wala*) of their attack, my age and height notwithstanding. Raj Bhai was wise enough to know that Vasoo Sir would not make any cricketing statement lightly, nor make a proclamation about the ability of a player without having weighed things up. If Vasoo Sir said something, it had to be true.

Vasoo Sir always had my best interests at heart. Take the time in 1987, when he was the India Under-15 coach and invited the legendary Mushtaq Ali for a visit to our preparatory camp in Indore. For the uninitiated, Mushtaq Ali was an opening batsman, and with his 112 against England at Old Trafford in 1936, he became the first Indian to score a century overseas. Had World War II not come in the way, Ali would have played far more than the eleven Tests he ended up with, and this is easily backed up by the fact that he played his last Test at the age of thirty-eight.

Vasoo Sir introduced me to Mushtaq Ali Sir and proclaimed that I was possibly the second-best batsman in India at that time, after Sunil Gavaskar. He said that he would be surprised if I didn't play for India in the next five years or so. Not too many coaches will make such bold predictions. But then again, not too many people have an eye for talent that Vasoo Sir was born with and has meticulously nurtured over the years. Though I always believed in my own abilities, that comment gave me more confidence and inspired me to make those words come true. It enabled me to set a bigger vision for myself—not only to represent India in international cricket but to become one of the top players in the world.

There is another hilarious story from the Indore camp. Vasoo Sir's son, Jatin, had also been selected for the same camp and was my room-mate for the entire month that we were there. After dinner every night, he would bowl to me with a plastic ball. (Knocking with a plastic ball can reduce a batsman's reaction time, which helps one when playing with the red cricket ball.) The noise made by the plastic ball— when it bounced off the surface and when it hit the bat— really irked the security guard. He asked us to stop, but we happily ignored his protests. Fed up with our refusal to stop playing, he went to Vasoo Sir's room and complained, 'A short boy is batting, and your son is bowling to him this late at night.' Sir told him, 'Why are you standing here? Go and field and help them.' Bemused by this, the hapless guard never bothered us again!

A crucial and pivotal juncture in my journey as a cricketer was the 1988–89 Ranji Trophy season and the 1989 Irani Trophy match between Rest of India and Delhi (the Ranji Trophy winners that season). After my successful first Ranji season for Mumbai, I was selected for this Irani Trophy match. It was also scheduled to be the selection match for the Indian tour to Pakistan. I was in the Rest of India team. We were playing at Wankhede.

I got into my stride quickly in the first innings but got out to Maninder Singh. In the second innings, I was well on my way to a century, but I was running out of partners. Approaching the end of the final day, I was 11 runs short of a century when Venkatapathy Raju was dismissed and the innings was considered all but over. The next man in, Gursharan Singh, had suffered a fractured finger in the first innings after being hit by a ball delivered by Sanjeev Sharma. Raj Bhai had asked him to go out to bat and help me reach my century. To his credit, Gursharan, who could not even pull a glove over his right hand, walked out to bat to assist me to the milestone. I was very touched by Gush's gesture and told him to block. 'I will tackle Maninder Singh,' I told him. The ball was turning but I was well-set and feeling good. With Gush at the other end, I got my 100. It was an important innings for me, and in a week's time I was on a plane to Pakistan to realize my dream of playing for India.

Vasoo Sir was watching this Irani Trophy match with my father. My father would never watch me play—he had this superstition that if he watched me play, I would get out early. But apparently, Vasoo Sir had convinced him to come to this game. Sir took out his 1955 Fiat and drove my father to the venue, telling him, 'Don't worry, he won't get out . . . If your presence was reason enough for him to get out, all the schools in Mumbai would want to hire you as their principal.' My father simply laughed and got into the car. I am forever indebted to Sir for this. My father watched me play live only on two occasions, and this was one of them. The memory makes me very emotional.

These aren't the only incidents where Vasoo Sir backed me. Before he got the ear of Raj Bhai, he'd told his fellow Dadar Union player, the then Mumbai captain Dilip Vengsarkar, to allow me to bat against the Indian team's bowlers. Although Vengsarkar had heard of me, he was understandably sceptical of letting me face Chetan Sharma and Kapil Dev. They were at their best, and there was every chance that they would prove too much for me to handle. But he agreed to Sir's suggestion. I remember batting in the nets against the great Kapil Dev, who was one of my heroes. This brief interaction with the Indian team bowlers gave me the opportunity to taste what international-level bowling could be like. I believe this became an incentive for me to perform well. These kinds of experiences boosted my confidence, and the encouragement and appreciation helped. I am told that after seeing me bat in the nets, Vengsarkar spoke to the Mumbai selection panel, and as a result of this I got selected for the Mumbai team. Vasoo Sir believed this exposure would help and encourage me, and he was already thinking way ahead of anyone else—thinking of how to help me succeed.

There are occasions in one's career when one has just come back from an injury. To ensure the injury doesn't aggravate, one curtails his game and starts prioritizing defensive play over natural strokes. I was going through one such patch. 'Sachin, patience is for players who don't have the talent that you have,' was the message Vasoo Sir sent me through Anil Joshi, who at one point of time managed Sungrace-Mafatlal's cricket team. Even though the comment was humorous, I took it very seriously, and I thought deeply about what Sir was trying to tell me.

Vasoo Sir never gave me any technical tips. I had a very unorthodox batting grip, with both hands way down the bat's handle. Achrekar Sir had tried to work on changing my grip, but since that hadn't worked for me he advised me to go back to the same grip. Vasoo Sir was aware of this and therefore didn't say a word about it. His suggestions were always around building an innings, analysing the opposition, studying the nuances of the game by thinking as a captain when you're batting, etc. This really opened my mind to what this beautiful game is all about. I realized then and strongly believe now that good coaching is not only about knowing how to coach; it is also about knowing when not to coach.

Vasoo Sir is one of the most understated people (like my coach, Achrekar Sir). He never once claimed any credit for any of his students, and that's what I respect about him— his ability to give as a coach without expecting anything in return. A few years ago, I invited him for the launch of my book and wanted to start off the evening with him, as he had seen my earliest days very closely. The first segment of the event saw Vasoo Sir, Sunil Gavaskar, Dilip Vengsarkar and Ravi Shastri chatting about my early days, with Harsha Bhogle moderating the panel. Sir was at his wittiest best and had the audience in splits. It was the best possible start to the evening. I remember calling Jatin a couple of times prior to the book launch, to ensure that Sir attends, knowing full well that he could be a tricky customer to get to these media events, as he prefers to stay low key.

'What I Saw in Sachin . . .'

I was told by Anil Joshi about this young boy who was supposedly a great talent. When I saw this boy bat, the first thing that jumped out at me was his reading of line and length. He played every ball perfectly—what had to be played off the front foot was played off the front foot, and the deliveries that demanded to be played off the back foot sent him deep into the crease! Such perfection I had never seen before in anyone that young.

I knew he was Achrekar's student, and I understood immediately that the boy had played hundreds of balls in the nets, thousands even. It seemed to me that he knew how to deal with any ball: it could be a shooter on a maidan outfield or a rearing delivery on a worn-out pitch or a wickedly spinning leg break—Sachin seemed to have seen it all!

The boy could also do everything else in addition to batting. Well into the later stages of his career, he had it in him to be a top-tier leg-spinner, with a googly that couldn't be read by many batsmen. He was a brilliant fielder, with possibly the best throwing arm among his contemporaries and even his seniors! But what for me was the clincher was that the boy wanted to score runs and more runs. Never at the cost of the team, though. He wanted to score those runs for his team to win! This was apparent to me right from the start. He had a very shrewd cricketing brain; in our circles we call it 'cricketing intelligence'.

Also, when I worked a little more closely with him, I understood that Sachin had another great power: the power to forget. He was able to erase the memory of the previous ball or the previous innings from his immediate focus. This is the factor that separates the greats from the non-greats: the ability to shut out what's happened in the past and stay in the present. This, to me, is one of his biggest strengths.

—Vasoo Paranjape

Cricket attracts its fair share of troubled characters. Not necessarily troublesome, but brooding, introverted individuals obsessed with a singular pursuit. SANJAY MANJREKAR is one of those, or at any rate was one of those when he still played the game.

Manjrekar had a name to live up to, that of the late, great Vijay Manjrekar. But the son is definitely his own man. Considered a technician of the purest form and adhering to the rules of textbook cricket, Manjrekar played some exceptional innings in his time, and in parts of the world where Indian batsmen did not always succeed.

And yet, for all the pedigree, Manjrekar would not have ended up following in his father's footsteps had it not been for the timely intervention of Vasoo Paranjape. In his book *Imperfect*, Manjrekar has been candid about the difficult relationship he shared with his dominant father. When it was time for Manjrekar junior to take a hard cricketing call and move to Dadar Union, it was Paranjape who convinced Vijay Manjrekar to allow the switch.

Manjrekar's links with the Paranjapes run deep, beginning with the obvious cricketing push that Vasoo provided but strengthening further with the affection and care that Lalita Paranjape bestowed on the young man when she took him under her wing. If today Manjrekar can look back on his career with such clarity, and perhaps be at peace with himself with regard to his cricketing past, it is in no small part because of the Paranjape influence.

The Best Thing That Can Happen
to a Cricketer

Sanjay Manjrekar

Almost anyone you speak to about Vasoo Paranjape will tell you about his sense of humour, which, of course, is legendary. What most people don't know is that the angrier Vasoo gets, the wittier he becomes. But he's not one to lose his cool. His understanding of the game, his reading of it, his genuine cricketing intelligence, made him stand out in the Mumbai cricket crowd. And, trust me, Mumbai cricket is the school of hard knocks, and it rightfully boasts more than its fair share of cricketers, experts, coaches, you name it. But Vasoo was at a very different level from everyone else.

For starters, the language he spoke was different. By this I don't just mean to refer to his excellent command of English but also to his understanding of the grammar of cricket. It helped that he always spoke his mind and never had any agenda other than the good of the game. He did not fear the outcome of what he spoke, he could never be a *chamcha* to anyone, and beyond a point, I think, he couldn't help but be straightforward, even if this meant being brutally honest. While Vasoo was a lover of cricket and of cricketers, he was never touched by sycophancy.

The thing about Vasoo is that he has impacted so many cricketers, including me, in such a significant way. But you will never hear him claiming that some cricketer is a product of his mentoring. As a coach, Vasoo had a light touch, and it was usually the finishing touch—just what you needed as a cricketer. He was not a long-term coach but rather someone who came into your life at exactly the right time, pointed you in the correct direction and then withdrew. He did not expect players to be in touch with him, but he would watch every ball on TV like a hawk, and you could rest assured that when you saw him next and went up to him, he would let you know whether your game was good or not so good.

The great quality in Vasoo is that he has a different outlook on life. Not just about cricket, you could have a conversation with him about music or movies, and you would still come away having learnt something. I remember the hours I spent at the Paranjape residence, where discussions around the lunch table would be of the highest level. I think it helped that the husband and wife—and you will know what Mrs Paranjape is like—came from different backgrounds. But they are a tremendous team. If you spend time with the two of them, you will realize that it's impossible to imagine Vasoo without Lalita.

I remember the time when I was doing well in cricket, making my mark at different levels, but falling behind in my studies. Mrs Paranjape called me out of the blue one day and told me, 'Sanjay, at 11 a.m. you will go here for math tuition. At 2 p.m. I've arranged for you take lessons from so and so. And at five o'clock you will report to so and so.' Trust me, besides the cricket that Vasoo taught me, Lalita played a major role in my development, and I can say without doubt that I owe both of them a huge debt of gratitude.

Vasoo's advice was never technical in nature. He would talk to the team—and to me—about game situations and his experiences from the past. His comments were mostly anecdotal and painted the bigger picture so well for us as a team. When he was around, I always went back home having learned something valuable. He was very smart and shrewd in the way he planned my journey for me, albeit I had very little knowledge of what was going on. He put me at the top of the batting order at Dadar Union when I'd just joined the club. This gave me the advantage of playing longer innings and scoring well in club cricket, paving the way for me to play for Mumbai. Also, since he got me playing for Dadar Union, he helped put two other heavyweight champions in my corner: I played alongside, and under, Sunil Gavaskar and Dilip Vengsarkar. Watching them bat was a huge learning experience for me, and having them watch and observe me play was an added advantage. Vasoo Sir also made me captain of Dadar Union, adding more strength to my cricketing résumé as I made my way to playing for the country. These were all shrewd moves by my well-wisher who believed in me. And it was all done without him saying a word about it to me.

There was always an air about him that made him stand apart. Of course, he was a handsome, good-looking guy. (And Jatin is fortunate to have inherited this, although he is a different personality altogether.) But Vasoo also ensured that he was consistently well-turned-out. I guess that was the Dadar Union way in some sense.

In those days, there was an air of stiffness about certain cricketers, especially when it came to dealing with newcomers or inexperienced players. But Vasoo was more chilled-out. Of course, he played hard and played to win. Of course, he chased excellence fiercely. But once the game was done, he was the kind who could unwind, drop his guard and have a laugh over a drink. He could get along perfectly well even with people who were, by nature, very different from him. V.S. 'Marshall' Patil was one such. Vasoo and Marshall argued about and debated virtually every subject under the sun, but their relationship was so strong that nothing could affect it.

I'm fortunate to have played with both Vasoo and Jatin, at different times in their respective careers, and I thoroughly enjoyed the experience. The thing with Vasoo is that he always has your best interests at heart. I remember the time when he had recently taken up umpiring and was participating in a Kanga League match. Dadar Union was playing on an adjacent strip, and every once in a while, when he wasn't watching his own game like a hawk, he would speak to me, adjusting my fielding position depending on the batsman on strike!

When India went to the West Indies in 2016, the great Viv Richards was commentating with us, as was Jeff Dujon, and the old stories were flowing. At some point, Ajay Jadeja mentioned that it would have been so fascinating to have Vasoo in the same discussion. During the break I called

Vasoo and handed the phone over to Sir Viv. Naturally, the two were perfectly comfortable chatting away, swapping stories. I was happy to have been able to make that happen.

I can say with confidence that Vasoo is the best thing that can happen to a cricketer. That proved to be true in my case. To give you another example: there was a bit of shilly-shallying about me playing for Dadar Union at first. Most people did not want to approach my father and to put that idea across to him. After all, you did not take liberties with Vijay Manjrekar, whoever you were. But Vasoo had absolutely no such qualms, and all it took was a five-minute chat between him and my father. I don't know what he told my father, but there is a rumour in Mumbai's cricketing circles that Vasoo had suggested that I'd become a good rummy player if I joined Matunga Gymkhanna, and that if I wanted to be a cricketer I should play for Dadar Union. And so, it was done.

I did not look at Vasoo as a father figure, because that was not what I was in search of. His impact was subtle, like a batsman playing a late cut or a leg glance—a deft touch here, a gentle push there—and before you knew it, you had grown as a cricketer.

'What I Saw in Sanjay . . .'

Sanjay's father was a close friend of mine, so I knew him from the start. Something about Sanjay told me he would play cricket. I went to watch him play an inter-school match at the Fort Vijay Cricket Ground at Azad Maidan. He scored a century. I think Dilip Sardesai's son, the journalist Rajdeep Sardesai, was playing for the opposition. Rajdeep himself was a good player, but I was there to watch Sanjay.

I immediately realized that the boy was a natural batsman. It was as though cricket was in his genes. He had that look of a good, solid batsman—an ideal number three. Everything about him seemed to have been cast in a batsman's mould. His head position was impressive, very correct, which is important at the international level. I also noticed that he took many singles, which to me showed that he had a plan for his innings.

I was determined that he should play for Dadar Union. He joined the club, and I wasted no time in batting him at number three. I also told V.S. Patil to keep a very close eye on him and work with him at the R.A. Podar College nets to iron out a couple of issues in his batting. Marshall (as V.S. Patil was called) was great at this, and he concurred with my view that the boy had immense potential. So we started working on him together.

Sanjay scored many runs for Dadar Union, becoming an integral part of the team. I handed him the captaincy pretty early on, so that he could improve his game faster and also get himself into the captaincy race for Mumbai. I was very keen on Sanjay becoming the captain of Mumbai and taking that big step towards playing for India. He was a very good thinker of the game and would always be mingling with the old guard at Dadar Union, including Shridhar Mandle, Subhash Kshirsagar, Avi Karnik and Suresh Tigdi. I observed from the sidelines that Sanjay was an out-and-out Dadar Union man. That gave me immense pleasure because I had literally forced his father to bring him to Dadar Union. I strongly believe that Dadar Union set the stage for his international career.

Sanjay had a fabulous international career, but I always wanted him to be more attacking than he was. I think he was such a big fan of Sunil Gavaskar that the defensiveness of the guru was also imbibed by the chela.

—Vasoo Paranjape

When he was a young batsman coming up through the ranks in Bangalore, RAHUL DRAVID was known as a destroyer of spin bowling. By the time he had established himself in domestic cricket and piled up the runs for Karnataka and South Zone to make it to the Indian team, he had grown into someone who handled quick bowling better than his peers.

His breathtaking stroke play or staunch defence really caught the eye of experts and spectators alike. As did his ability to concentrate hard and spend hours at the crease. Dravid became known as a technically accomplished cricketer—one who played copybook cricket.

Keki Tarapapore was Dravid's long-time coach, right from his early days to his glorious run for India. But along the way there were others, too, who stepped in and gave Dravid the push he needed to take his game to the next level. One such figure was Vasoo Paranjape, with whom Dravid attended a month-long under-15 camp in Calcutta, in 1988.

The Empathetic Coach

Rahul Dravid

Whenever I am asked about cricket coaching—and I am relatively new to this role—one of the things I say is that today, it's a new world, and for youngsters finding their feet in the game there's a new normal. The challenge that coaches face these days has to do with the retention of players. If you go to a grassroots academy, people there will tell you that 50 per cent of the kids who attend a summer camp don't come back again. The dropout rate in India is high. We don't think about it a lot because there are so many other kids coming through.

But the fact remains that so many players have left the game. It's not that all of them would have become cricketers, but if you are a coach you have to think about how to keep people in the game—if not as players, then as spectators, as consumers of the game. You want to keep people involved in the sport, and that's the challenge ahead of coaches in India today.

Some of the kids, if they have the wrong experience with the game early on, end up not just leaving cricket but turning their back on sports in general, and this is dangerous. As a coach dealing with someone who is just starting out in a sport, you need to give your students a grounding in the game while at the same time making it interesting and fun for them.

A lot of the older coaches used to do this intuitively: finding the passion and energy in a kid and making them realize the necessity of commitment and practice. It's a fine balance. As a young person, if you want to learn this game, if you want to groom your basics, you must practise, you must do a lot of repetitive drills, which is not always fun. It's not an easy game to learn. Though there aren't too many fundamentals to worry about, the few basic skills that are absolutely essential to cricket need to be mastered early on.

In this, the coach's role is absolutely vital. You have to be able to spot it when kids are going wrong with their basics. Senior coaches—who watch the game day in, day out—pick up on these nuances much quicker than anyone else. They didn't have video technology in their time, so they had to rely on their eyes, depend on their instincts, and that gave them a great advantage.

Previous generations—mine included—learnt a lot of cricket looking at photographs. Keki Tarapore would always have the *MCC Coaching Manual* handy, and we would look at a certain photo illustrating some cricket shot, play the shot in our head and work out with our coach how to actually go about attempting the shot in the nets. You don't obviously need to do that now, because you have the advantage of video technology. But in this new scenario coaches need to be smart enough to sense when something is going wrong and intervene at the right time, especially when dealing with young players.

As you deal with a relatively older group of players, like I do, the scope becomes broader. Now you're talking about tactics and strategy, about how and where to score runs. The questions you are asking are also slightly different: What do I need to develop in my game to make it more effective? How do I deal with pressure? How do I deal with success and failure? The coach-student equation completely changes. But—and this is going to sound repetitive and boring—all of it has to be built on a solid foundation of getting the basics right.

As a cricketer, you need to know how to adapt but also how to get back to the basics when required. This is the major advantage of having a Tarapore or a Hanumant Singh or a Vasoo Paranjape as your coach. They followed your game when you were a kid and they followed it when you became an established player. They could always remind you of what you did when you played well, and they could make you aware of what was missing from your game at a certain time.

In those days, we learnt a lot through discussions and conversations about cricket. When you have the time to flesh things out, offer opinions and counter-opinions, have animated debates, you learn things without even knowing it. In our time, there is so much to look at, so much tech at hand and so much structured video analysis that discussions about technique and cricket don't happen as much as they used to. And that's a pity.

My month with Mr Paranjape? Well, he had a huge reputation in the game and I was only fourteen years old at the time. What I remember from that month was his sheer passion for cricket. He was truly, deeply in love with the game. We'd have a morning session and an evening session, and we'd go home in the middle for lunch or whatever, but he wouldn't leave the ground. He might take a nap in the dressing room, but he was right there. You saw the excitement in his eyes when we did well. If a young bowler was swinging the ball or spinning it hard, or if a batsman played a cover drive, it genuinely made him happy. At that age, the lightest pat on the back from a coach like him made all the difference to me.

For a boy of fourteen who wants to absorb as much as possible, learn as much as possible, there's nothing more important than a source of inspiration. And for me, that month was all about getting inspired. After it was over, I walked away thinking, 'Hey, this is the standard I've seen in players in India. I'm probably not there yet, but I need to get there, and I can do it.' If I want to be good at cricket, I said to myself, then I am going to need to develop a passion for the game.

I also felt reassured because Mr Paranjape never gave me the sense that he was intervening too much technically or interfering with how I tried to play the game. I was the second wicketkeeper in the group. I could bat a bit, but I was there primarily as the second wicketkeeper. And I was told by both Mr Paranjape and Hanumant Singh: 'You're going to play for India, but not as a wicketkeeper.'

When I attended an under-17 camp a year later, Hanumant Singh took me aside for a chat and told me to look in the mirror and think hard about whether I wanted to keep or not. Back in those days the wicketkeeper typically batted at number six, so the chances I got were also limited. I was fortunate to score 70-odd in a zonal match where I ran out of partners. Then, someone in South Zone saw something in me and moved me up the order. So coaches have been very crucial to my growth as a cricketer.

Coming back to the subject of coaching. One of the differences between the old approach and the new one is that today you have to pay attention to larger groups of players than previously. You have to think about kids who are not as good as those to whom the game comes naturally or easily. You have a duty of care to everyone in the group. It is impossible to give everyone the same kind of attention or opportunities, but at least in your mind you have to be aware of that duty of care. As long as you have that as your philosophy, your guiding principle, you'll be okay. Of course, you will get things wrong and won't be able to keep everyone happy, but that's not how you judge a success or failure in coaching.

It's also important to recognize the stresses and pressures that children are under now. They choose cricket as a profession early on, and the decisions you take about them could be life-altering. It's not easy but you have to take those calls. In a country like India, more and more kids are taking up cricket every day, the pool is getting wider and a lot more talent is emerging from smaller towns and cities. This can lead to a situation wherein a player may be very good at his level or in his local circuit but may struggle to get opportunities at a higher level, simply because there are other players who are better than him. A coach has to handle such situations with empathy, understanding and care.

There have been coaches working at the grassroots level—men like Ramakant Achrekar, Paranjape, Hanumant and Tarapore—who gave their lives to the game. Tarapore got paid by the Karnataka State Cricket Association but it was not a significant amount, and from the Bangalore United Cricket Club he drew nothing. And yet he was there every day. He was the first in, to ensure the nets had been put up, the matting was in order; and then we would show up, have a session and head off to school or college or whatever, but he would still be there, making sure all was as it should be. First in and last out, every single day. And that did eventually take its toll on his health: he had to have his leg amputated owing to complications caused by varicose veins. The impact and influence of such coaches cannot be measured.

It is no wonder that Bombay of a particular era was such a dominant force for such an extended period in Indian cricket. The strength of Bombay cricket was built on the shoulders of these coaches and was the product of their passion to promote and nurture young talent. It would be fair to say that in those days, a cricketer from Bombay had his basics and fundamentals covered better than cricketers from other parts of the country. This was because of these committed coaches, who were also selflessly investing their time and efforts into clubs, colleges and schools.

As cricket gets bigger, more people are getting into coaching as well, and what worries me sometimes is the quality of these people that the game is attracting. That is where the influence of someone like Paranjape—who inspired me first as a cricketer and inspires me now in my coaching career—comes in. Back then, knowledge was power and it made people like Paranjape so invaluable. But today, in our world of video and YouTube, knowledge is easily accessible. So what is of crucial importance now is the quality of people imparting that knowledge. Are those who guide us today as inspirational—through their words and deeds—as those who guided us in the past?

Becoming a coach has had a definite impact on me. It has enabled me to see things a little more holistically and to have more empathy for the players; it has taught me new things about myself and allowed me to learn more about younger players; it has forced me to put myself in other people's shoes and look at the game as they might. When you're a professional sportsperson, you are thinking so much about your own performance and what you can contribute that you get into a bit of a tunnel-vision mode. Coaching has opened that up for me completely.

'What I Saw in Rahul...'

He came as a keeper-batsman, and I requested him to focus on his batting. I also wrote to C. Nagraj, the Karnataka State Cricket Association secretary at the time, to ensure that coaches in Karnataka also follow the same approach with him if possible. Rahul was a very disciplined and serious boy, always first at the nets and hanging on to every word that was said to him. He also had a natural cricketing brain, and I remember thinking that he would make a good captain, albeit a very studious one.

He was always a batsman who valued his wicket, even as a young player, and he was very classy and 'neat' in the way he went about his batting. You could see his hunger to play a long innings, and I was confident that with Keki Tarapore as his coach in Bangalore, he was in solid hands. I tried to touch up his game a little, without doing anything drastic with his technique, not that anything drastic needed to be done. I emphasized on building an innings and other tactical tools to help him approach innings and match situations better. I also stressed that it was extremely important that he enjoy his batting.

—Vasoo Paranjape

One of India's greatest match-winners, ANIL KUMBLE has many achievements to his name: he has taken 956 international wickets, pulled a ten-wicket haul in an innings, went on to captain India and even scored a Test century. Post his retirement, he served as the president of the Karnataka State Cricket Association before becoming the coach of the Indian team.

Kumble's first interaction with Vasoo happened at a camp in Kolkata. This cemented the bond between the mentor and the mentee. Not only did Kumble make it a point to call on Vasoo whenever he was in Mumbai—and this continued deep into his career as an international player—but he also wrote letters to Vasoo from time to time. Yes, the old-fashioned way, on inland letter cards.

Sample this letter, sent by Kumble on 7 January 1989, more than thirty years before he sat down to look back at his relationship with Vasoo:

Dear Sir,

How are you? Sorry for not writing to you earlier. I got a seat in R.V. College of Engineering (mechanical course), which is one of the best colleges in Bangalore University.

This season I got wickets for my college in the Inter-Collegiate tournaments and for my club in the league matches but I did not get much of batting to do since all the matches played here are limited overs.

To my darn luck I could not appear for the Under-19 and University trials because, while playing a match on November 2 at our college grounds, I twisted my right ankle and tore a ligament while fielding. My leg was put in plaster cast and the doctor told me that he would remove it only after three weeks. But at the end of the third week I developed high fever and the doctor confirmed typhoid. I suffered for 17 days and in the last week the temperature has come to below normal but I still have not recovered completely.

The doctor has advised me not to play cricket for at least three months and diet is also restricted.

Gopalakrishna is getting lots of runs this season but unfortunately he wasn't selected for the Under-19 state team.

I hope I will make up for the loss this year. Wishing you a very happy New Year.

Yours truly,
Anil K

This is a priceless look into the mindset of one of India's most competitive cricketers, and serves as a portrait of the match-winner as a young man, if you will. What comes across in it is a sweetness that you would never have associated with Kumble once he became an international cricketer—a hardened professional who snarled at obdurate batsmen and raged when teammates misfielded off his bowling. But such

Modelling days: Vasoo Paranjape during a shoot for Oberoi Hotels, in the 1970s.

Vasoo as an eighteen-year-old, after scoring 130 for Elphinstone College at an intercollegiate tournament in 1956

Featured on the cover of *Sport and Pastime* magazine.

With Arun Wagh (*left*) at the Khar Gymkhana Tournament in Mumbai.

With two of the all-time greats of Indian batting—Vijay Hazare (*right*) and Sunil Gavaskar (*left*).

Trying to make a point to Mohammad Azharuddin during the 1987 World Cup camp in Delhi.

Dadar Union's Kanga League-winning team (1970–71 season): '*This picture was taken at my favourite cricket ground, the Cricket Club of India in Mumbai.*'

Purshottam Shield 1974 winners: Dadar Union. This was Dilip Vengsarkar's first year at the club—he is seen standing right behind the trophy.

With the CCI team
on the Kenya tour
in 1978. A young
all-rounder named
Kapil Dev (*fourth from
right in the back row*)
made people sit up
and take notice
during this tour.

Vasoo with
longtime friend and
cricketer Rohan
Kanhai (*left*).

'*With Ramakant
Achrekar, who I
thought was the best
batsman to play in the
Kanga League.*'

With Dennis Lillee and Jeff Thomson at the MRF Pace Foundation, Chennai.

'Dennis had to listen to a lot of anecdotes during our time together.'

With W.V. Raman (*left*) and
Dennis Lillee.

With Sir Viv Richards at the
D.Y. Patil Coaches Conclave in
Mumbai, 2013.

'*With Azhar and my dear
friend Raj Singh Dungarpur.
This was the classic expression
he would have on his face when
passionately discussing cricket.*'

'With my two favourites—Sunny and Dilip.'

With the India Youth team before departing to Australia for the 1987–88
Youth World Cup.

'With my wife, Lalita, and Sachin at his retirement function.'

With Sir Garry Sobers at cricketer Madhavrao Apte's house.

The Paranjape family at Vasoo's seventieth birthday celebrations.

was his relationship with Vasoo that young Kumble felt comfortable enough to open up to him in this manner.

And while Vasoo certainly showed Kumble the ropes, in terms of technique and skills, it was not as though his role was limited to that of a coach. Their relationship was not a formally defined one, as between a teacher and a student. A lot of learning and teaching happened between them in an unstructured manner.

Time for a Chat

Anil Kumble

He sat on a chair in his impeccable whites. The famous floppy hat fitted perfectly on his head. As a youngster from Bangalore who had travelled all the way to Srinagar for an India Under-19 camp, I had goosebumps when I went up to greet him and introduced myself: 'Hello sir, I am Anil K.'

He spoke to me first about the basics of spin bowling. Simple things like how to cock your wrist, how to time your jump in your run-up, when to pause . . . And I wrote all of these things down on the back page of a diary I carried with me at the time. I wish I had that diary today.

It was really helpful in that he was very methodical in the way he spoke about the game. The way he spoke about skills and technique influenced and helped me at a young age.

I was initially selected as an all-rounder. He worked with me on my batting, but he also realized that I had to bowl slightly orthodox to be useful going forward—and that was a struggle for me. But he had given me a direction at a young age.

My conversations with him were useful because I got a lot from his knowledge of the game (not just how to play it but how it was being played at the time), his experiences with the system and his stories that are folklore.

Ultimately, as a cricketer you are basically collecting information from everyone. And then you have to utilize what is good for you. At the end of the day, only you know what is good for you. You try out things, see if something is working and then add it to your game. The coaches you remember are those who have given you something that improves you as a player.

It's not that you fall back on one person. Ideally, you should be able to absorb ideas from all the coaches you speak to. And even more important is watching others play—your teammates, your opponents—and learning from them. That's what influences and shapes you.

Vasoo was very disciplined. He let people know if things were not being done as he expected them to be done. These factors are key in the development of an individual.

It was not just about cricket but also about what Vasoo stood for. He made sure that we didn't limit ourselves to cricketing discussions. It was about life. Daljit Singh, when he became the coach of Karnataka, had a similar influence on me—he made me think about fitness, life and the other things around the game. You may not realize this at the time, but in the long run these are the conversations that have an impact on you.

The chat at the end of a practice session, at lunch, at dinner, at a gathering: it's getting rare these days. There are too many distractions, too many other things that people are occupied with. Players have their own dedicated time for themselves. These days, since there is a lot more cricket happening, you barely get any time for yourself. So the coaches today realize that players need their space. But for us, personal time was meant for having chats.

The current generation does have opportunities, in some ways more opportunities than their predecessors had. There's IPL, there are foreign players who have a positive influence on our cricketers. There's also a lot more unstructured and informal activity, owing to a lack of formal channels of communication. Cricketers are trying to understand the history of the game and are learning about former players. But they're not having as many conversations.

I often go back to those conversations. As a coach, I have realized that after a point cricketers tend to get confused if you focus just on their skill set. At the international level, there is hardly anything you can add to your skill set. There are times when you have to tweak a little, come up with a new variation, work on a new stroke. But it really comes down to understanding your own self; understanding the challenges that come with playing day in, day out; understanding the pressures of playing professional sport—the pressure of performance, the pressure of fitness. How do you overcome these challenges? By having conversations with people. That to me is more important than skill development.

You need to look at the older generation and learn from them, just as they learnt from their predecessors. They have a passion for the game and can teach you a lot about what went into the making of cricket and what goes into the making of a cricketer.

Cricket may have changed, but it's still about bat and ball; you still have to score runs, still have to take wickets. How do you bowl a certain ball, how do you mark a batsman, when do you set a certain field, how to plan an innings? You never know when, while conversing with your seniors, you might get that one tip that will help you.

'What I Saw in Anil . . .'

When I first saw Anil, I thought an academic was walking towards me. He had a very 'soft' air about him, gawky and tall with big, framed spectacles. When I saw him bowl, I was instantaneously impressed.

There was an unerring accuracy to his bowling, ball after ball. He made the batsman more and more watchful with every single delivery of his. For a leg-spinner to be so accurate was a huge advantage. I knew I had to work with him around this fulcrum of accuracy.

Soon, I realized that Anil also had a tremendous hunger to succeed. He was determined to becoming better and spent a lot of time with me, discussing spin bowlers and other subjects. I made him bowl to every batsman at the nets, every single day. Not once did he complain or have a frown on his face. He wanted the hard yards. His hunger to succeed was the other asset—apart from his bowling—that I thought would help him in his career.

I once told him, 'There can be another B.S. Chandra.' I told him to stick to his natural, faster pace and not fall into the mould of a normal spinner with slower pace. His speed was his advantage and his deliveries, thanks to his height, generated steep bounce from the surface.

He was very reserved and did not speak a lot, but he hated being hit by a batsman. I could see it in his eyes. The next ball he delivered after being hit was usually much quicker than usual, putting the batsman in a spot of bother almost always. His aggression was unspoken, his tenacity was unspoken, his hunger was unspoken. I knew India had a winner in him, if nurtured properly.

Anil was lucky that Ajit Wadekar was his coach during his formative years playing for India. Ajit has such a terrific eye for talent, and he knew Anil was his match-winner, ensuring that the right path was paved for him. I watched joyfully from the sidelines as Anil made a name for himself on the greatest stage of cricket.

—Vasoo Paranjape

This boy from Borivali could bat, but he did not get much of a chance to show it in the two practice matches that were held for the under-17 squad in Mumbai. ROHIT SHARMA came to bat late in the one game where he made it to the crease, and he then had to swing merrily away. The kid was worried that he would not be able to impress those who were watching, and he shared this concern with his coach, Vasoo, when he had a moment. This was what Vasoo told him in response: 'Don't worry about getting chances. You play your game and enjoy it.'

Rohit is a happy-go-lucky chap. He's not what you would describe as the typical *khadoos* Mumbaikar. He stands tall at the crease like an Englishman when he drives through cover. He has the backbone of a dinkum Australian when he pulls, hooks or shimmies down the pitch on his toes and launches a spinner fifteen rows deep into the stands. Rohit is an exceptional cricketer, but he would not have broken even into the Mumbai eleven if not for Vasoo.

All the while Vasoo had been talking Rohit up to those who needed reliable information on emerging talent, he was telling the batsman that, talented though he was, there was more to the game than scoring runs and winning matches.

Rohit made 60-odd in his first Mumbai Under-17 match and a century in the next. In Baroda, where Rohit made his first century, there was a local man watching the kids play: Kiran More, forever called Jockey by his friends because he was so vertically challenged, was the chairman of the National Selection Committee.

We now know Rohit Sharma as an astonishingly successful cricketer. Since 2015, he has been the pre-eminent Indian batsman in limited-overs cricket, overshadowed only by Virat Kohli. Rohit has 9,115 ODI runs to Kohli's 11,867; averages 49.27 to Kohli's 59.33; has 29 centuries to his skipper's 43; and has therefore been forced to play second fiddle. But these numbers, nonetheless, are staggering.

When you stack on to the stats the fact that Rohit has had the privilege of leading the Indian team only in Kohli's absence—when several other key players are also resting—it brings to the fore his ability to handle the resources given to him. If Kohli is the more naturally ruthless run-scoring beast, Rohit is the better captain. Whether it is about picking the right eleven players who will give their cricketing lives for their skipper, about giving bowlers the fields they want, or about choosing when to choke the run flow and when to aim for a wicket—Rohit is always ahead of the game, as any captain should be, and well ahead of Kohli.

And his leadership skills, too, can be traced back to his days as a young cricketer. From being among the thirty probables for the Mumbai Under-17 team, Rohit swiftly made his way to the playing eleven. After only one season, he was picked for the India Under-17 squad and was then fast-tracked into the Mumbai Ranji Trophy team. And here, too, Vasoo had done his deft little bit.

Rohit had a meteoric rise in the Mumbai Ranji Trophy team. The stripling was playing with the likes of Vinod Kambli, Wasim Jaffer, Ajit Agarkar and Amol Muzumdar. And now, there was no Vasoo Sir to steer him through the choppy waters. But the confidence he had gained from his previous interactions with Vasoo, during that one season in Mumbai, made him flower into an international cricketer— it was enough to ensure that Rohit could hold his own in any dressing room.

A Father Figure

Rohit Sharma

I remember very clearly when I met Vasoo Sir for the first time. There was an Under-17 camp at Wankhede Stadium, and out of the thirty probables only fifteen were going to make it to the team. When you're a kid trying to make your mark in Mumbai cricket, you're more focused on what you have to do at a trial than on learning about people who are watching you. I knew they were all respected coaches, especially Vasoo Sir, but I had no clue about what cricket he had played or which players he had mentored.

Soon after, Vasoo Sir was in conversation with Pravin Amre, who was the chairman of the Junior Selection Committee; he was telling him about me. When Amre Sir started to talk to me about Vasoo Sir and explained who he was and what he had done for Mumbai cricket, I was dazed. I realized that this was a massive opportunity for me. Here was a man whose knowledge of cricket was amazing, and whose mind bordered on cricket-crazy, and I had a chance to absorb what I could. I decided to make the most of this opportunity—to learn, to glean as much as I possibly could from Sir. This was my big moment!

Though he mainly had to focus on the playing eleven, I kept trying to find some excuse to be near him and talk to him. Actually, I just wanted him to talk, so I could listen and learn. Remember, we come from the Bombay school of cricket. There is a standard that has been set and these are the people who have done it before us—they played with legends and won everything, every season.

He watched me during one of my net sessions at Wankhede, and then something happened. He went to the captain and said, 'We need to get this kid into the team. You figure out your combination and all that. I won't interfere. But this boy needs to play. Work with me.'

Prashant Naik, who was the captain, came to me. 'Look,' he said, 'I don't know anything about you and I've not heard much about you either, but Vasoo Sir says you have to play. So you're playing tomorrow.'

When I scored a century in an under-17 game in Baroda, I remember Vasoo Sir talking to Kiran More about me. Vasoo Sir saw some spark in me, and he always made it a point to push my case.

I got to learn from him how to approach batting in different situations. He always told us: 'No two situations are the same. Try and read the game—where you are, what you can do for your team and the situation your team is in. Learn this as soon as you can because now is the time to learn, not when you are playing for Bombay or India.'

In so many of my innings for India, there have been instances when I have thought of something that Sir had told me all those years ago and applied that to the present game.

When I first met him, I had only played one season of junior cricket. I had no concept of playing for Mumbai or India. But here was this person telling me what I should do, urging me to take small steps ahead. Young players sometimes get overawed and forget that the big things happen only if you do small things perfectly. This is something he always did, as I later realized.

When speaking to young players, he knew how to get them to move forward, one step at a time. There is no point telling youngsters about bigger goals at that early a stage in their careers, and he understood that. This is what you call a helping hand. This is just what young sportspersons need.

When I go out to the middle, I remember the things Vasoo Sir told me back then. Things like: as a batsman or a captain, if you can't read the situation, the team is already in trouble; if you're the boss, you have to walk out like you mean it, otherwise the shoulders of those who follow you will droop.

He treated all of us like his own children, not as cricketers. We never felt that we were training under a coach. He was more like a father figure to us. He never uttered an aggressive word, projected no negativity. We lost games, there were people who did not perform consistently, but he never spoke to them harshly. He was always polite and friendly, and that's what you need at that age. I was lucky to have played under him.

I felt no pressure despite the fact that I was playing in the Mumbai atmosphere. All our lives we had been told that if you don't win the title, it's not a successful season. We were always reminded of the high standards set by those who came before us. All of us had to play with that in mind. But I can confidently tell you that not for one moment did we feel any pressure from the management, coach or selectors, and that was because of Vasoo Sir. He would speak to all of them, listening carefully to what they had to say and then tell them, 'Don't worry, I'll take care of it.'

He protected us from everything. He got negative feedback from selectors, officials, journalists and others, but he just kept it all to himself. We also heard these things. But when he came to us, he never mentioned a word. It was all batting, bowling, fielding, solving problems.

It's very important to be able to demonstrate a skill, especially to younger guys, when they're just not getting it. The worst thing is for the coach to send the wrong message. If a player does not understand, Vasoo Sir would not let him go. If he had to pick up a bat and get in the nets to show the player just how something should be done, he would do that.

Our team was the Mumbai gang. But Vasoo Sir could talk to us in Hindi, English, Gujarati and obviously Marathi. Apart from those, he could also speak other languages: fielding, batting and bowling. Everyone got what they needed from him, whether it was information or technical input.

Even today, I look forward to any message from Vasoo Sir. Jatin, who has always been around, is my bridge. I always ask him, 'Anything?' I know Vasoo Sir watches my games when he can and, trust me, any input he gives me is gold dust. After every innings I wait to hear from him, and if he can't get through to me because I'm travelling, I wait for Jatin to get in touch.

I blossomed as a cricketer in that one season with Vasoo Sir. Whether we won or lost, he would sit us around and talk about the game. After these sessions, we let it all go and went to sleep with a light mind, shedding the baggage and thinking about what we needed and wanted to do the next day. He freed my mind, allowed me to dream about playing for India and showed me the steps I had to take to get there. That's what Vasoo Sir does to a cricketer.

When I look back, I realize how shrewdly Sir had forged the path that led me to the world stage of cricket. I was not from a big club or a big school or a college team. I was an outlier. But Sir's recommendations to Pravin Amre, Kiran More and Dilip Vengsarkar got people talking about me, and I delivered on that promise. Without Sir by my side in those early years, I would not have been able to achieve as much as I fortunately have.

'What I Saw in Rohit...'

When I first saw Rohit, what struck me was how easily he was able to middle the ball. As a batsman, a big part of your ability is that X factor of timing. Timing is all about meeting the ball at the right moment to enable maximum impact, and Rohit had that ability in abundance. I could immediately see that he had the raw material to play at the highest level. His head was also extremely steady, and I remember I would exhort him to concentrate harder, to watch the ball more closely, especially after it pitches. He was a carefree lad, and I knew I had to give him some direction. I thought the best way of doing that was to try and get him to concentrate harder—to make him realize that batting is not only about hitting boundaries and looking pretty, but also about having to put your head down and being very disciplined when the situation, the pitch or the bowling demanded it.

He was also an extremely good fielder, with great catching hands and a strong arm. This was a big plus point, as you cannot hide on the field in international cricket. Another big advantage was that under his carefree exterior, he had a streetfighter element in him, which added a whole new dimension to his game. The number of international hundreds and runs he has scored is testament to that fight in him.

I often spoke to him at length about game situations and about how he needs to think like a captain when he bats—a mindset that automatically brings more discipline into one's game. I remember he used to bat at number seven in the Mumbai Under-17 team, and I ensured that he was promoted up the order, to the top four. He responded well to the promotion, by scoring a big hundred, and never looked back after that! He has also developed into a very shrewd captain, cut from the same cloth as many of the shrewdest Mumbai captains before him.

—Vasoo Paranjape

YUVRAJ SINGH was arguably India's most destructive limited-overs batsman of all time—someone who was dead serious about his game. But he is also a natural joker, a prankster, a leg-puller and the kind of person who can be described as young-at-heart irrespective of the age. So it's understandable that Yuvraj not just took a liking to, and developed a fondness for, Vasoo but also listened closely when the old man spoke. Vasoo was a coach he could look up to in more ways than one.

The coach-pupil relationship is an extremely unusual one in Indian cricket. In the beginning, it is a one-to-many relationship. The coach has to attend to many students initially. As the players develop, the men are separated from the boys and more attention is paid to those most likely to transition to the next level. When a young child picks up a bat or ball, it is the coach who draws the lines on that clean slate, determining what sort of cricketer the child would grow up to be. But after a while the balance of power shifts.

When a player has made it to the top, to the highest level of the game, and is playing for India, this relationship becomes many-to-one, with multiple coaches claiming a stake in the successfully baked pie. By this time, the rookie has become a professional, has seen fair-weather friends, fake well-wishers as well as genuine goodwill, and has generally gone through the ups and downs that any adult faces in the process of growing up and making a place of their own in the world. But it helps to be pointed in the right direction when you are most vulnerable.

Yuvraj has had his fair share of brushes with coaches at different levels in his life. But Vasoo's influence on him was formative. Once, in a match early in his Ranji Trophy career, Yuvraj misfielded a ball—it went through his legs and made it to the boundary. There were shouts of 'India Gate' at the stadium. That taunt hurt him enough to make him want to be the best fielder in the country, and for a period he was. Although tall and slightly lanky, Yuvraj had the fast-twitch muscles that enabled him to move rapidly over short distances, the long fingers that made catching a pleasure rather than a pain and a shoulder that fired Scud missiles.

It was Vasoo who'd made him realize the importance of fielding. Vasoo himself was one of the pioneers in this area, having taught Indian cricketers the importance of fielding at a time when it was considered unfashionable to get your whites dirty and unwise to dive on grounds that were far from conducive to such acrobatics. From the maidan matches of Dadar Union to the Ranji Trophy games at Wankhede and elsewhere, Vasoo was a stalker on the field, always looking for an opportunity to make an impact on the game.

Yuvraj went on to play 304 One Day Internationals, 40 Test matches and 58 T20 Internationals. He was the Player of the Series when India won the World Cup in 2011; he hit six sixes in an over off Stuart Broad in an ICC World T20 that India won; and over the course of his career, he became one of the most dominant middle order and lower-middle order batsmen India has ever produced in limited-overs cricket.

But all this didn't come easy for him. Imagine the shock of being pulled out of your bed at two in the morning on a winter night in Chandigarh. The icy winds blowing off the hills sending chills through your bones, irrespective of how many layers you have on or how warm your blanket is. And if getting out of bed is a shock to the system, consider what it is like to have to change into cricketing whites at that hour before stepping out to the backyard, where a net session awaits. The light is dim, the surface is hard concrete and in the cold of dawn, even a slight brush of a cricket ball will sting like a bullet and leave a bruise that will change colours.

This was a part of Yuvraj's life at the hands of his most influential coach, his father Yograj Singh. Once a teammate of Kapil Dev, Yograj's dreams of a glorious international career never came to fruition, and he was determined to ensure that his son would do him proud.

It's common knowledge that Yuvraj barely liked cricket when he was a child. Roller skating was his first love, the one physical activity that gave him the most joy. (Once, when he brought home a roller-skating medal, the father was quick to throw it out.) But over the years, Yuvraj grew to love the game he was born to play, much as Andre Agassi had, overcoming both his hard upbringing and the take-no-prisoners approach of an overbearing father.

Learning to Love the Game

Yuvraj Singh

I had never ever met a coach like Vasoo when I got to the National Cricket Academy in 1999. I'm not saying anything bad about the coaches I had till then—the people who helped me reach my potential. I would never do that. But, till I met Vasoo—I would call him 'Sir' but he always told me not to—I never imagined that a coach could also be like this.

I was very young back then and did not know too much about the game; I hadn't had much exposure. Even my English was not that great. I was not comfortable speaking in a formal way. And to listen to the way he spoke English was a different experience for me. All those stories about Bradman and Sobers were something else for a simple guy from Chandigarh. But he made me feel so comfortable. I still don't know how he did it. It wasn't just about the language, because his Hindi was good enough for us to communicate. But he had a way of disarming you, making you feel like you had known him all your life. And the jokes—oh, man, the jokes!

One of the things I learnt early on is that those who know a lot about batting technique say very little about it. When you were batting in the nets and Vasoo was watching you, he would say the simplest things: 'Watch the ball, Yuvi'; 'Wait for it, Yuvi'; 'Don't try to hit it so hard, Yuvi'. Only later did I realize that he was making technical adjustments to my game without me knowing it. If he had told me, 'Take this stance . . . pick up the bat like this . . . swing the bat like this . . .' there would have been natural resistance on my part, simply because I was used to doing things a certain way. But when he asked me to watch the ball longer, he was actually working with my feet, making me wait that extra second before committing to the shot, When he told me not to hit the ball too hard, he was ensuring that I got my timing just right.

The most important thing I learnt from Vasoo is that there will always be a hundred people telling you what to do, how to do it and when to do it. Advice is free in this country, where everyone is a cricket expert. But, just as a coach chooses which player to spend the most time on, which one is likely to come good, so as a player you need to be able to figure out whom to listen to and whom to ignore. It's like going to a buffet: most things will be tasty and tempting, but some are better for you than others. Vasoo used to just lay it out like that and then allow you to make your mind up. He never forced his opinion on a cricketer.

While training, I never enjoyed fielding drills. Let's be straight, it is the most boring part of any cricketer's training regimen. Take 100 high catches, 100 in the slips . . . It's just the wrong way to do things because it's totally different from what happens in a match situation, no matter how hard you try to replicate it. But Vasoo made this into some kind of personal challenge for me. He was never the kind to say I was doing badly, but it was clear from his reaction when he thought I could do much better. After that, I felt that I had a duty to make sure I did not let him down.

If I had known more about Vasoo back then I would have definitely become a better cricketer at a much earlier stage in my career. But I can say this for sure: what I learnt about myself, about the game, about how things worked—I couldn't have without Vasoo. You have to remember that this was 2000–01; the world was a different place. There wasn't so much exposure, there wasn't so much out there you could tap into, and as a cricketer you were pretty much in a bubble, looking to score as much as you could in the next match to help your team to win and obviously, to help yourself move to the next level.

I remember a match at the Buchi Babu Tournament in Mumbai, between NCA XI and Indian Airlines. I was in the middle, and I hit the spinner Sunil Joshi for a big six; the ball couldn't be found. A message came from the dressing room, telling me to take it easy. I knew it was from the NCA XI coach, Vasoo. But I was batting well at the time, seeing the ball well. The pitch was pretty flat, and I was feeling good about my game. We needed a big score. So in the next two overs of Joshi, I hit him for three more sixes—each of those balls was lost.

And then, when I came back to the dressing room after getting out, Vasoo did not say one negative word to me. He did not ask me why I did not listen to him when I was instructed to settle down and take it easy. He did not criticize me even once. All he said was, 'You've wasted four perfectly good cricket balls. Whether it goes over the ropes or into the river, you only get six runs.' The whole dressing room broke out in laughter.

I may never have learned to love cricket if it were not for Vasoo. I was good at playing, but it's well known that I did not really love the game when I was growing up. My father was sure he would make me a cricketer, even when I was more into roller skating. But without Vasoo, I would not have fallen in love with cricket. And when you love something, you can put your heart and soul into it—not for one day or one week but day in, day out. There were so many times when the game knocked me back. So many times I got dropped from the Indian team. I never really got a consistent run in the Test team. To make a comeback each time required commitment and hard work, and also belief. Without Vasoo, that would never have happened. I just would not have had the mental strength.

I am happy with the chances I got in my playing career and with what I was able to do to contribute to the game— whether it was at the under-19 level, for Punjab, for India or in the Indian Premier League. This is just a game, but for many of us it is the most important part of our lives. So, to love cricket without it taking over your entire being you need to have balance. And Vasoo taught me how to love cricket without getting obsessed with it. I owe him.

'What I Saw in Yuvraj . . .'

Left-handers please the eye more than right-handers. When I first saw Yuvraj at the first National Cricket Academy camp in 2000, I immediately knew that he had something special. He was a naturally strong lad, and he innately possessed the unique gift of timing. I could sense that here was somebody who could be groomed into a real asset for India.

My first assessment was: he stood tall and used his reach well, but not well enough. I started having regular conversations with him to understand how his mind works. He had played many cameos in his career, but that's all they ended up being—cameos. He had much more in him than he himself realized at the time. He was a potential star and needed to be looked after . . .

I was keen on him batting at number three and had promoted him, for the Buchi Babu Tournament in 2000, ahead of another promising player, Mohammad Kaif. Yuvraj promptly scored two big hundreds and was on the plane to Nairobi for the ICC Champions Trophy.

I spoke to him about tempering his innings at the crease, about the need to think about the team and harnessing his ability for the good of the team. I remember he took those words to heart and scored a hundred in the Buchi Babu final.

He could field brilliantly at point and also had a brilliant throwing arm. On top of everything else, he was more than useful as a bowler when required.

—Vasoo Paranjape

AJAY JADEJA played 196 One Day Internationals for India, batting mostly in the lower-middle order. He also scored four half-centuries in a fifteen-Test career that might have been much longer if he had worked out earlier just how to make the most of himself as a long-format cricketer. Here was a player who understood the game better than most, an all-rounder who joined the team when India was searching for the next Kapil Dev. While Jadeja loved every moment he spent on the cricket field, he wasn't quite sure just what he was. Batsman? Bowler? All-rounder?

Today, he is remembered as the only player who had this unique ability to not only see things that others miss, but also to look clearly at what was right in front of you and correctly guess what it might become. And he got that ability in large part from Vasoo Paranjape.

A Cricket Coach and a Life Coach

Ajay Jadeja

I had not heard of Vasoo Sir before I landed up at an India Under-17 camp in Srinagar in 1987. You can understand what knowledge a sixteen-year-old had of former players in those days. I was so involved in my own world, thinking only about how many runs I would make and wickets I would take, about whether or not I would get selected for the next tournament. At that age, you can't help but focus on yourself.

We first met at the ground. It was a breathtakingly beautiful venue, and as a player you were on a high merely owing to the fact that you were there, having been selected.

People who know Vasoo Sir would have experienced his sweet nature, his unique personality. He is driven by an urge to help others improve their game and to teach them how to enjoy the game; he wants to share his joy of cricket. This was evident when I first met him. He had his cigarette, his shorts, his floppy hat—any young player would have been in awe at the sight of him. And I will never forget the floppy hat . . . There are some images that make an impression on your young mind and stay with you forever.

He was not what you'd call a cricket coach as is understood in today's world. For us he was, and is, a life coach. Cricket was the medium and the language, because that was the only thing we young idiots understood at the time. We did not know of anything beyond; our world was so small. So he used cricket to connect with us and talk to us. I've seen him talking to raw sixteen-year-olds and to Dennis Lillee and other senior cricketers with the same level of involvement.

After spending only one month with him, I couldn't grasp what he was really about. If at that time one of my friends had asked me what the coach was like, I would've stupidly said: '*Mumbai ka tha, thoda sa paagal tha, magar unme woh cricket ka keeda tha* (He was from Mumbai, was a little mad, but he was bitten by the cricket bug).' I was too enamoured of the floppy hat and the cigarette drooping from his mouth. That's all I understood back then.

In those days, I was an all-rounder in the sense that I couldn't really bat, couldn't really bowl, couldn't really field, but I did as much of each of these things as I could when given the chance. If it were not for Vasoo Sir, I would still be just as confused. Spending time with him made me think about myself, about my game and about how I might fit into a team.

What we understand by the term 'coach', and what we expect from a coach—Vasoo Sir was that too. He did not tell us about the ninety-eight-degree angle the bat came from, nor about whether the loading arm was working or not when bowling . . . He did not speak the language that experts spout today. Instead, he spoke to us in a language we understood. Without using all that jargon, he sorted us out anyway. Over the years, he taught you how to focus on many more things than just technique. That's possibly the simplest way of putting it. What he provided to us was not coaching, not lessons on technique, but a philosophy.

When he came across a promising player, he liked to spread the word. He talked about Tendulkar, Ganguly, Kambli . . . He would harp about Tendulkar and describe his cricket with such admiration. He'd say, 'Two years you watch this boy, Ajay. He's special.' Now you understand why he said that.

At that under-17 camp in Srinagar, I asked Vasoo Sir which player he thought was special and could go on to play at higher levels. That's when he spoke about Anil Kumble, who would get more runs than all of us in that camp. Anil was a good batsman and was doing his job there, so that's what we saw in him. But, honestly, none of us thought of him as a great bowler. You really would not have thought there was anything exciting about this cricketer. But Vasoo saw things differently. He saw things in cricketers that nobody else could.

Because he had a vision, he could see things in a different light. We would sit around and say, '*Buddha paagal ho gaya* (the old man has lost it)' and have a laugh. To us, Kumble was a batsman and a brilliant gully fielder who bowled a little. But Vasoo Sir had this special eye, and I'm blessed to have seen what he was showing us then, has shown us since. (I spoke to him recently about Twenty20 cricket, and he sees a future for it.)

He had certain parameters to assess cricketers: skills, fielding, fitness, personality—he would not eliminate anything. He added to you as a cricketer and as a human being. That is Vasoo Paranjape.

How did he help me? Arré, just like he helped everybody. He was never bound by questions of language or region or even country. The language of cricket goes beyond different states, different zones, different countries. And he taught you how to learn that language without restricting yourself to any one school of thought. There are two ways to coach. Either you hand down a syllabus, demand obedience and tick all the boxes, or you can tell someone: 'This is where you need to go. Let's go on that journey together.'

'What I Saw in Ajay . . .'

Ajay came to Srinagar for the National Camp as a sprightly lad with a bounce in his step and an air of carefreeness about him. He was a naturally attacking batsman, always looking to score runs and play shots. He was a very natural fielder too, who was excellent at anticipating where the batsman was trying to play the ball. But more importantly, he loved fielding and was passionate about it. I've always felt that as a fielder, it is very important for you to take a lot of pride in your abilities and to take it as a challenge that no ball should go past you. Ajay had that mindset, in my opinion. He could also bowl medium pace, but he bowled more to remain 'in the game' than anything else.

—Vasoo Paranjape

At the Mumbai Cricket Association in Bandra Kurla Complex, RAMESH POWAR, the former India off-spinner and coach of the women's team, sets down his cup of tea because he is overcome with emotion. Tears flow freely, and after a while he composes himself deliberately and carefully, much like be bowled his beautifully tossed-up yet devastatingly dipping off breaks. He is moved because he cannot speak about Vasoo without becoming emotional.

Powar, chunky even as a child, used that heft to good effect in his game. He batted in the lower-middle order, and he never took his bowling too seriously until Vasoo made him realize his talent.

One of the worst times in Powar's life was when he had been dropped from the Mumbai Under-19 and the Police Gymkhana teams. He had fitness issues and nobody was willing to sign him up. He was all set to quit cricket and maybe opt for a safe government job in his attempt to move forward in life.

It wasn't just cricket that had tripped him up. Back then, he had just lost his father, and his family had to move out of their government quarters. With no real source of income and no immediate prospects, his future looked bleak.

Being down and out taught Powar two things. First, that he had to take charge of his own destiny. Second, that cricket was his ticket to better things. And he credits Vasoo for making him realize both these truths.

When he was at the crossroads of his life, what Powar needed, more than anything else, was a person who could show him a way out. Not quite light at the end of the tunnel but baby steps that had to be taken in order to open doors. Vasoo never told Powar what to do, but he did shine a light on the things that helped him to overcome his situation and taught him how to look towards the future with optimism rather than dread.

From coaching promising youngsters in the Mumbai circuit, Powar made the transition to coaching India's women's national team in 2018. Many eyebrows were raised at the time as he had never coached a team at any competitive level before getting this international appointment. But Powar was not deterred. Not very long ago, he had heard all the whingeing, taken all the barbs and come through as a cricketer.

Today, Powar is not just older but also wiser, harder and smarter than the young man who'd almost turned his back on cricket. What's more, he will be a cricketer's cricketer till his dying day, as well as a coach's coach—because he absorbed all that is good about the game from old man Vasoo.

The Man Who Changed My Life

Ramesh Powar

Without him, I would not have become a cricketer. Without him, I would not have been here, talking to you.

My first interaction with Vasoo Sir happened when I got selected for the Elf Vengsarkar Academy. I had seen him before, but I didn't know how experienced a coach he was. As I began to play better cricket and spoke to more of my seniors, I got to know just who he really was and what impact he'd had on the game.

I was picked in the Elf Academy as a batsman. I liked him instantly because unlike other coaches, he wasn't always talking technique. Other coaches were always telling me about my stance, grip—things like that—and about what changes I should make. Vasoo Sir was positive from the word go. If you hit a six, he would clap and not tell you to play along the ground. It was clear that he liked cricket and cricketers.

When the bowlers were tired I used to bowl in the nets. Vasoo Sir would stand behind the net from start to finish—

nowadays you hardly see that—because he was convinced that a coach had to give time to bowlers (also when they batted). I enjoyed bowling. He watched me but did not tell me how to bowl off spin, how to turn the ball more, how to flight the ball. He just told me one thing: whatever happens, don't stop flighting the ball. 'You might get hit, you might get wickets, but stick to your strength.'

Looking back, I realize just how brave a decision it was on his part to invest time, money and effort in me at that time. I was nowhere in cricket. Not just nowhere, I was a nobody. And for Vasoo Sir to put efforts towards my development at that stage—it is staggering to even imagine that. It shows his thinking. Because I am a coach now, I understand just how much of a leap of faith it must have been for him. But he did not stop there. While he did not push me towards batting or bowling, he convinced Dilip Vengsarkar and Makarand Waingankar that 'this boy' was not just a batsman. I used to come in at number six or seven and score attacking half-centuries, so the team was happy with me.

Vasoo Sir was the one who helped change the way people looked at me. When someone backs you like that—in a scene that had other cricketers like Sairaj Bahutule, Nilesh Kulkarni, Rajesh Pawar and Rohan Hirlekar, who were all taking wickets consistently—your confidence naturally goes from rock bottom to sky high. While I thought I was a nobody, Vasoo Sir had faith in me. I won't call him my guru, because a guru is someone who just teaches you. To me, he is much more than that: a guiding light that appeared in my life at the right time. Without him I would have been nowhere.

Early in my career, I made the rash decision of leaving MCA Colts to play for another team. A lot of people questioned my move. My brother told me that I had made a mistake—and he had played for Mumbai, for India Under-19 . . . My friends told me that I was doing the wrong thing. But Vasoo sir never told me I was wrong. He still saw enough in me to back me. I cannot tell you how important a role he played in my life at that time. He taught me how to enjoy my bowling, how to respect myself. Nowadays, you see coaches shouting from the rooftops that they have coached X or Y India cricketer. Vasoo Sir has never once done that. His love for cricket was selfless.

In six months Vasoo Sir made me believe that I was a bowler, and that is the only reason I stayed in cricket. I had an offer from Central Railways—I had a job and I could've easily given up cricket. We did not own a house at the time, and after my father died we had nowhere to go. I was ready to give up everything, my dream of playing cricket on the big stage, my ambition of taking the wickets of the best batsmen in the world . . . I was ready to close all those doors and just focus on helping my family financially. It was the worst time of my life. I was, for all practical purposes, down and out. Vasoo Sir was not only the person responsible for the turning point in my cricketing career; he was the man who changed my life. Whatever cricket I played, as a spinner for India, as a Test cricketer, was because of him.

I visit Ramakant Achrekar Sir every Guru Purnima to pay my respects to him. But I don't do the same with Vasoo Sir, not because I don't respect him as much, but because our relationship is different. Neither does he expect any cricketer to give him credit or touch his feet, nor does he treat youngsters as though they know nothing. If you are a cricketer, you are dear to him. I don't think he would like it if I came to meet him formally in that manner. But every Mumbai cricketer knows where to find Vasoo Sir, whether in Matunga West or at the CCI or elsewhere, and you know you can meet him casually. There's no need to make a special thing out of it. I once did that when I was playing for India, making a point of seeking him out, and he almost ticked me off. He said: 'You're playing for India now. Don't question your own abilities and come running to me.' I got the message then and there.

The values and principles I have absorbed from him—the need to practise hard rather than looking to please or impress people; the importance of performance; respect for the game—these are the lessons I have learnt. The greatest thing is that he never came to you and told you these things. Just the way he conducted himself, the way he behaved and the way he steered us in a particular direction was enough.

The greatest thing about Vasoo Sir? Not once has he said, 'I made Ramesh Powar the cricketer he is.' Not once has he said that he was the coach of Ramesh Powar. That is how he is: never taking credit, never claiming to have done something. That's what makes him my original guru, my teacher, and that's what enables me to properly understand, without sentiment, his influence on my life. I can say, hand on heart, that without Vasoo Sir there would have been no Ramesh Powar.

Vasoo Sir doesn't just love cricket. From the time he wakes up to the time he goes to sleep, he lives cricket.

When he meets you, he meets you as a friend, treats you as a human being, as an equal. When he is at the ground, he sees only batsmen and bowlers, spinners and fast bowlers, wicketkeepers. I'm not the only cricketer whose life he has touched, that's for sure. And every cricketer who has had the good luck of being under his wing knows, deep down, that he is who he is, as a cricketer, as a professional, because of Vasoo Sir. It would not have happened if our paths had not crossed with Vasoo Sir's. He will be embarrassed if I thank him, so I will not take that path. Rather, I would thank God for sending this man to my life when I needed him the most.

'What I Saw in Ramesh . . .'

The first day I saw him bowl at the Elf Academy in Mumbai, I was taken aback. I had been told that Ramesh was a batting all-rounder. But from what I saw, he had three important attributes that go into the making of a quality off-spinner (or any spinner for that matter). He bowled from close to the stumps, bowled the right line and flighted the ball. But as he started working with me and as I saw him happily take the higher workload of bowling to each and every batsman in the nets every single day, I realized that he had one more quality which was his key strength: he had a big heart, and that's why he never stopped flighting the ball. It did not matter whether he got hit for a six or a four, he kept flighting the ball as he had a plan in place.

I worked with him on what the right fielding positions should be for different kinds of batsmen and in different situations. I also interacted with his captain and coach at the Mumbai level to explain, and align them to, the fact that this was a different sort of bowler who had to be treated with care.

He was extremely hard-working, and I am so pleased that he went on to play for India with distinction, doing what he did best: flighting the ball!

—Vasoo Paranjape

W.V. RAMAN is likely remembered as a tall, attractive left-handed batsman who became the first Indian to score a limited-overs century in South Africa. A Tamil Nadu stalwart, he played eleven Tests and twenty-seven ODIs for India, a tally that many believe should have been much higher, given the quality of his batsmanship, his skilled slow left-arm bowling and, most importantly, his sharp cricketing brain. In December 2018, Raman was appointed the coach of India's women's national team and took them to the final of the 2020 ICC Women's T20 World Cup in Melbourne, where Australia once again emerged as the top team in the women's game.

If you sit down with Raman to talk cricket, you would understand why he gets along so famously with Paranjape. The two are birds of a feather—both have an intense love for cricket, a quiet passion to absorb its intricacies and a firm understanding that the game is bigger than anyone who has played it. Raman has got to know Paranjape over a lifetime in cricket. At first, it was as a player seeking contact with a more enlightened mind; then as a former cricketer who was still tied to the game; and now, as a fellow coach, as someone trying to pass on a bit of what he has learned over the years. It is no surprise that the two get on so well.

The Coach I Would Reach Out To

W.V. Raman

Vasoo conveyed his ideas in a special way, by speaking to you as a friend, not as anything else, irrespective of his position and yours. The other thing, which many people underestimate, is that he helped rid you of whatever fatigue or tiredness you had as you walked off the field.

When you were practising or doing your training routine, he would help ease the tedium of that activity. But don't get me wrong. With him, you always knew where you stood, what your goals were and what you had to do. He had a unique way of getting the balance right, between life and cricket. He could always tell you a lot in terms of what you had to do with your game, but beyond that, he could bring in humour, get to the heart of things with a caustic word, which was never meant to hurt you.

He was somebody you could turn to at any time of the day—you could literally call him at midnight and he would be there for you—and this made him very, very special. That was the kind of commitment he had to the game and the kind of responsibility he felt towards cricketers. It was as though he could not help himself and always wanted to be there for you.

I first interacted with him in the mid-1980s, and from there on our relationship became something else. He was what you would call a fund of knowledge, or rather an ocean of knowledge. Not only did he grasp the intricacies of your game, but he could also talk about the game as it was played before you arrived on the scene, if you were interested in knowing that. For us, he was a walking, talking *Wisden*.

As a player, the one thing I would always ask him was what he saw in my game. Back then you did not have video analysis and other assorted technologies at your disposal. So you placed your trust on somebody who actually watched your game, rather than on a contraption. He watched me play regularly, and since he had the eyes of a hawk, he could spot the deviations from the norm in any player's game. He could tell you what you were doing differently now as compared to when he'd seen you two or three months earlier.

The best thing was that he would tell you what was now different in your game and happily leave it at that. Once he had told you what he had observed, it was up to you to ask for further suggestions. He would never offer unsolicited views or advice.

Vasoo was such an experienced coach even when I was playing. He understood the importance of giving his inputs at the correct time. A piece of advice can only be absorbed by a player when he is in the right mental space and needs to know things from a coach. Vasoo was aware of that, and so he always waited for the player to ask for help.

Once I finished playing cricket, our relationship evolved into friendship, thanks to Vasoo. It was a riot whenever we met. We used to speak about everything under the sun, especially about what was going on in cricket at the time. I found much pleasure in nudging him towards his humorous gems, and he never let me down in a single conversation. This is a quality people should know about: Vasoo will never, ever let you down in any way.

If you go back to his gems, the humorous things he has said over the years, you will probably have to compile a separate book just for that. All too often, his humorous take on things lightened the mood while shining light on some greater truth. Here's one that I can share right away.

When we met soon after the Haryana versus Mumbai Ranji Trophy final in 1991, Vasoo was quite clear: 'Dilip [Vengsarkar] should have known that Abey [Kuruvilla] is the second-worst batsman on earth.' So I sheepishly asked, 'If Abey is the second-worst batsman, who is the worst?' Vasoo said: 'Arré yaar, it's the roller. It can only roll—it can't bat and can't score runs.'

You need to remember that this is a person who would never speak ill of a cricketer. He was not putting down Kuruvilla in any way. Rather, he was explaining the game and how the result panned out—Mumbai was bowled out for 352, chasing 355—in one typically humorous line.

Vasoo had a knack for figuring out what needed to be said when, to whom and in what way. But just because he spoke informally to you, almost as a friend, did not mean that he allowed you to take advantage of that. Another way of looking at it is that you, as a player, did not try to take advantage of his goodness at any stage, because if you did so you would be the ultimate loser. You did not give him 'yes-sir-no-sir' respect because he was a coach and you were a player, which is part of our Indian tradition and culture. He commanded respect, never demanded it, because he was that good.

I've worked as a coach a little now, and one of the things I believe in—something that Vasoo also always stood for—is that you do not try and change the fundamentals of a player's setup. You work within the framework of the player's technique and style, and you encourage him to become the best he can within those bounds.

The hallmark of Vasoo's coaching was that he was always positive. He could come across as sharp, condescending or acrid in the way he expressed himself when being humourous, but to only focus on that is to miss the point entirely. At heart, he has never run down any cricketer in his life. He has the same intensity and commitment when he is talking to a Gavaskar or a Tendulkar as when he is talking to a youngster. The only thing Vasoo is thinking is: 'How can I help this cricketer?'

Speaking of commitment, I remember a conversation between the late Raj Singh Dungarpur and Vasoo. Raj Bhai, as we all used to call him, asked Vasoo: 'What happens to us if this game is cancelled tomorrow?' And Vasoo, without batting an eyelid, simply said: 'We will commit suicide. What's left in life without cricket?' That's his commitment to cricket. It may sound like a cliché, but he lived his passion in every sense of the term. Don't try to challenge him on that.

Whenever I am in Mumbai, I try to look Vasoo up or at least call him, because we have developed a bond over a long period of time. He has been kind and generous enough to allow me to be a friend of sorts, but I have never forgotten the wisdom he brought to my life when I was still playing cricket. I'm thankful that he also seems to have enjoyed my company over the years and that he treats me like a friend, but I will always remember that he was already a great coach when I was playing. That wall of awareness will always be there between us, and I will take no liberties with him. Though he has given me the freedom to speak with him in a certain way, I will never forget the fact that he was the coach I would reach out to when I was a player.

Do you know who T.A. SEKAR is? Probably not. Because he played well before your time, when there was no Internet, no 24/7 television channels and cricket was not India's national pastime.

So here are some facts: Thirumalai Ananthanpillai Sekar is six and a half feet tall. He was one of the quickest bowlers India ever produced. He shared the new ball with Kapil Dev. He played forty-four first-class matches, taking most of his 130 wickets for Tamil Nadu between 1976 and 1990. He once took 9 wickets in an innings in a match against Kerala. He played for India, bowled with heart and hostility but did not get the results he might have and was dropped.

While international cricket may not have given Sekar as many opportunities as he would have liked, he was far from done with the game. Even as he was finishing his playing career, he turned to coaching, becoming the man in charge of the MRF Pace Foundation in Madras (now Chennai) under the guidance of Dennis Lillee, the undisputed guru of fast bowling. Sekar would later serve the game as a national selector from the South Zone and go on to take up coaching jobs with the Mumbai Indians and the Delhi Daredevils in the Indian Premier League.

The MRF Pace Foundation was set up to remedy the biggest bugbear in Indian cricketing history: a lack of genuinely quick bowlers. Not wily swing bowlers, not skilful seam masters, but actual fast bowlers. The Foundation worked at the grassroots level, looking for players who were between the ages of fifteen and nineteen. But they were faced with a challenge. How were they to find the right kids for the job?

Enter Vasoo Paranjape. Back then, Vasoo was the Director of Cricket at the Board of Control for Cricket in India. And Sekar depended on him for talent-scouting.

There was a time when many hopefuls came to the MRF Pace Foundation simply because it was the go-to centre for cricketers in India. The most famous alumnus was a vertically challenged boy from the Sahitya Sahwas residential complex in Mumbai. He initially tried to learn how to bowl quick but ended up instead as a world-class batsman, scoring nearly 35,000 international runs for India. His name: Sachin Tendulkar. Lillee had rejected Tendulkar, just as Vasoo had singled out many others—Ajay Jadeja, Sourav Ganguly—who mistakenly aspired to fast-bowling stardom when they were too young to know any better.

Good Times with Vasoo

T.A. Sekar

Whenever we spoke about Bombay cricket, the first name that would come up was Vasoo's. When I played for India, Sunil Gavaskar, Dilip Vengsarkar, Sandeep Patil were all products of Mumbai and were closely associated with Vasoo. Gavaskar and Vengsarkar played for Dadar Union, so they were much closer to Vasoo, who was highly rated by them and others as a cricketing mastermind.

In those days, there was a certain rapport between Mumbai and Chennai cricketers that was as hard to explain as it was impossible to deny. People used to tell young cricketers: talk to Vasoo. If you were from Chennai, you had no senior players for mentoring and guidance. There was S. Venkataraghavan, but every youngster was too scared to approach him. So we all used to talk to Vasoo whenever we got the chance.

I first met him one-on-one in 1986, when I was recovering from a knee injury. He asked me why I hadn't been playing more, and I told him about the injury. Immediately he got involved, instructing me to travel to Mumbai to meet a surgeon who had just returned from America. Vasoo introduced me to Dr Anant Joshi, who went on to become the most sought-after surgeon in India's cricketing circles.

When we wanted to set up the Pace Foundation, there was so much scepticism and opposition. From Bishan Bedi to Kapil Dev, some of the biggest names in Indian cricket were doubtful about what we were trying to do. But Vasoo believed in us. We roped him in as a consultant because he was an encyclopedia of junior cricket. Dennis called Vasoo the 'pocket *Wisden*', because the little man knew everything about cricket that was worth knowing.

Vasoo was a boon for the Pace Foundation because he would send the right boys to us at the right time. You won't believe it, but he knew about how each boy had performed in every match. He could reel off how many wickets someone took, what the situation was, what the opposition was. With Vasoo on board, the resistance to the Pace Foundation reduced. He was our bridge to the cricketers who had doubted what we were trying to do.

In fact, what Vasoo did was more than bridge that gap. While I was the one in charge of the Foundation, I was hardly in a position to speak with the youngsters who came largely from north India. With my Hindi and their English, there was no chance of interaction. So Vasoo helped us in this area, but he was more than just a translator. He could be speaking to Lillee one minute about Victor Richardson, and the next minute you could see him chatting in Gujarati with a fifteen-year-old from Rajkot, making the child feel at ease.

Vasoo spoke many languages, but most of all he was conversant with the grammar of cricket. He taught me how to love coaching. Many players are passionate about playing but find it hard to pass on their knowledge to the next generation. Vasoo took me under his wing and brought me to Mumbai to visit the homes of his favourite coaches. I met Vasant Amladi, who was kind of a coaching guru to Vasoo. I spent evenings with V.S. 'Marshall' Patil.

Think of your average day in an average week. Once you have spent hours at your job and minutes with your family, would you take the time to ensure that a young coach met the best minds of your generation? Would you facilitate these meetings and see to it that everyone got along? Vasoo did that, and with such acts of generosity he changed the lives of more cricketers than you might imagine.

Ajay Jadeja, Sourav Ganguly, guys like this came to the Foundation when they were young. Vasoo took one look at their game and told them: 'You can bat in our nets as long as you want, but please don't think we're going to select you to bowl.' He could take a look at a player for one session and make the call. That's how good Vasoo was.

Let me tell you another story. In 1985, when we were playing One Day Internationals against England, there was no talk of L. Sivaramakrishnan. But, in the gap between the ODIs we played a Deodhar Trophy match, and there Vasoo told Gavaskar about LS. When we were back in the Indian dressing room, suddenly LS was all anyone spoke about. Such was Vasoo's influence. And I knew then that if a fresh Tamil Nadu player was going to be picked, the other one— me—was out. LS played three Tests in that series.

Vasoo's sense of humour was so famous in cricketing circles that we all knew about it even before we met him. But there was one exchange I must share with you. This was at a Wills Trophy tournament played in Jamnagar, with Vasoo coaching one of the teams. There was a guy who knew palmistry offering a palm reading at the ground, and K. Srikkanth was the first to jump at the opportunity. 'Look at my hand, there are hardly any lines, nothing to worry about,' he told the guy. But before the palm reader could even respond, Vasoo told Cheeka, 'Listen, you may not have any worries, but when you are at the crease and swinging your bat, the rest of the team has to worry.' And that was not all. Cheeka was out of the Indian team then—this was around 1989–90—and he told the palm reader, 'I don't know why I'm not getting selected.' Vasoo butted in, saying, 'Don't worry about not getting selected now. We are all wondering how you got selected in the first place.'

One night, we settled down for dinner at the Park Sheraton in Chennai, at about 10 p.m. Lillee, Ian Chappell, Vasoo and myself. It was like watching a talk show. One story from Ian, one from Vasoo, and that was one hour gone. Ian hated Bradman, Vasoo loved him, and they would talk about every series from 1862 to 1997 and analyse them. At 2.30 a.m. the waiters came to us and asked if we were planning to leave, as they had to set up the restaurant for breakfast the next day. We asked for five more minutes, a beer and a rum. The next thing we knew it was 3.30 a.m., when the same waiter was back asking when we might finish. At 4.15 a.m. we left the restaurant and continued the conversation for another hour standing at the reception of the hotel. By the time I reached home, the sun had already risen.

If you want to have the best cricket evening of your life, call Vasoo over, sit back, relax and let the good times roll.

This Charismatic Man . . .

Dwarkanath Sanzgiri

(Author and journalist)

If I were to be marooned on a desert island, and God were to ask me to choose a companion to discuss cricket with, I would, in a heartbeat, choose the one and only Vasoo Paranjape.

In my twenty-five-year career as a cricket journalist, I have discussed cricket with numerous big and small players, as well as with the greats of the game. But there is no one like the inimitable Vasoo. He is truly one of a kind! He is God's designer product, never to be replicated.

If I had the choice, I would rather have listened to Bradman's cricket anecdotes not from Bradman but from Vasoo, for Vasoo loves Bradman more than Bradman ever loved himself. Even Sir Don wouldn't have been able to embellish or spice up his cricket stories as Vasoo can.

I would have enjoyed watching Sir Frank Worrell's batting and Vinoo Mankad's bowling sitting by Vasoo's side.

Alas, that was not to be! I missed that chance as I was born too late! Had Vasoo been a poet, he would have penned odes and encomiums to the great Sir Frank, immortalizing his stylish gait and his colourful persona. If God were to ask Vasoo whether he preferred to be born as Bradman or as Worrell in his next birth, Vasoo would be on the horns of a dilemma for sure. That would be a tough choice for him!

Vasoo's opinions are generally very strong. His views are his own and he expresses them fearlessly. He is candid, upfront but never offensive. Once, while interviewing him for a TV show, I asked his opinion about a left-arm spinner from the '80s. His response was, 'It would have been almost impossible for him to beat the great Weekes, Worrell, Walcott twice in a day. Bowling them out would have been an altogether different story. Remember the wickets of the '50s?'

I had not watched Vasoo much in his playing days. However, I had seen him captain his beloved Dadar Union team on the Mumbai maidans. Handsome, agile, he played with a handkerchief tied around his neck and stood out even among the greats of the game. His handkerchief became a hallmark, and many of us copied this style while playing in the narrow alleys (galis) of Shivaji Park. But that was as far as we could go; we could never aspire to be who he was.

At a time when fielding was not valued much in Indian cricket, Vasoo laid great emphasis on fielding and was a fielder par excellence. In this day and age, fielding is of paramount importance and gets the prominence it rightly deserves. So in this respect, Vasoo was ahead of his time. He moved with lightning speed on the ground and was undoubtedly one of the best fielders in the country.

Many of the key Dadar Union players in those days were confirmed bachelors. Vasoo broke this tradition by marrying early! With his brilliant sense of humour, he dispelled the grim air and high seriousness that prevailed in the Dadar Union dressing room and instilled in his team a spirit of camaraderie, joy and laughter. He created a sort of family feeling in the team by addressing his senior teammates by their first names and giving nicknames to the young players. So, Dilip Vengsarkar became Colonel; Suresh Tigdi, Major; Milind Rege, Minky; Sunil Gavaskar, Sunny; V.S. Patil, Marshall; and so on . . . And those names have stuck!

I met Vasoo in the '80s, when I was a budding sports journalist. That was a time when cricket lovers were fiercely attached to the Bombay Ranji team. If Bombay lost the prestigious Ranji Trophy, these fans would go into mourning until their team regained it the next season. In those days, I wrote for *Lokprabha* and that being a rare lean time for Bombay, I questioned Vasoo about what was going wrong with Bombay cricket. After having several chat sessions with this charismatic man, I was completely bowled over by the depth of his cricketing knowledge and his intellect. Over a short period of time, I learnt so much about this great game that I ended up enriching my own cricketing knowledge.

Somewhere down the line, Vasoo and I became good friends. I stopped using the honorific 'sir' and slipped into the familiar 'hey Vasoo' or 'arré Vasoo'. We have spent so many wonderful evenings on his terrace just talking cricket. Lalita and the kids, too, would chip in. Time has flown and today his children have all grown and are well-settled, with families of their own. Even today, the thought of meeting

Vasoo makes me happy. There has never been a day when I was bored in his company. In fact, if you ask me, there are only two cricketers who never lost their 'form': one was Sir Don and the other is Vasoo.

Who is this maverick persona called Vasoo Paranjape? What has shaped him?

He was never a great player and he knew it! He is self-effacing and unassuming. He never speaks about himself; I don't recall even ten sentences he might have uttered about himself. But when it came to appreciating others, he would draw on his rich vocabulary and his great stock of knowledge. Once, Ajit Wadekar had scored a memorable knock of 324 runs in university cricket. Vasoo, his partner at the other end, had scored a century. But I don't recollect Vasoo saying a word about his own ton; all he did was gush about 'Ajit's marvellous stroke play'. It was as if he knew more about Ajit's batting chart than about his own.

I have met several Mumbai cricketers who talk a lot about themselves rather than letting their game speak for itself. Many of them, ordinary cricketers all, have spent their lives whining about the 'injustices' they have suffered. On the other hand, I've never heard Vasoo utter the words, 'I was unjustly treated.' He uses his words to appreciate others. When he wants to be critical, his barbs do not wound; they are delivered so humorously that even the receiver joins in on the laughter.

As a cricket coach, he was highly revered. His coaching was not of the conventional, technique-based kind but rather flexible and inclusive. As Milind Rege always says, 'Sunil [Gavaskar] was not a good fielder initially. When

Vasoo realized that he had the makings of a great player, he encouraged him to concentrate on fielding and made him understand how important fielding is at the highest level of cricket. He groomed Dilip [Vengsarkar] too, loving him like his own child.' At various levels, Vasoo has been responsible for shaping and moulding some of India's top cricketing gems—right from Sunil Gavaskar to Sachin Tendulkar and Prithvi Shaw, he has influenced them all, Sanath Jayasuriya and Roshan Mahanama included.

Vasoo is a keen student of cricket history. He is widely read and has in-depth knowledge of the growth and development of cricket in the modern era. He knows everything about the various stadiums around the world, and he knows which bowler has taken how many wickets from which end of a particular stadium. I won't be surprised if he even happens to know the name of Wally Hammond's neighbour! He draws the right inferences and lessons from the sport's history and applies them to contemporary cricket. For instance, he advised Narendra Hirwani to wear a long-sleeved shirt while bowling. Why? The legendary leg-spinner Subhash Gupte used the sleeves of his shirt to conceal the grip of his googly. Vasoo has such comprehensive knowledge of the nuances of the game.

Vasoo's style of advising players was totally original. When Sandeep Patil left for the Australia Tour in 1981–82, Vasoo's cryptic advice to him was, 'Sandy, watch Lillee closely for the first thirty minutes. Believe me, he'll be watching you for the rest of the day.' This doesn't need to be deconstructed any further! Only Vasoo is capable of handing out such succinct advice.

His sense of humour is out of the box too, especially when it is deployed to admonish people. I was a witness to the following incident that occurred during a match. After scoring a delightful century, a well-known Mumbai Test cricketer played an irresponsible shot and threw away his wicket. He came and sat beside us. Vasoo asked him what happened. And he replied, 'It's so bloody hot.' Vasoo, with an utterly deadpan expression, hit back with, 'Why don't you play carrom instead? You can sit under a fan and play.' All of us, including the batsman, burst out laughing. Such flimsy excuses were not acceptable to Vasoo! On another occasion, a batsman told Vasoo that he had got out to an outswinger. That remark was a half-volley for Vasoo's wit. He quipped, 'If there was no outswinger in the world of cricket, Len Hutton would have scored 235,000 runs.'

Some things are anathema to Vasoo, like shoddy fielding, faulty running between the wickets, not shifting the bat from one hand to the other while running, getting into the crease without dragging the bat into the crease ahead of you . . . These things annoy him and lame excuses are never tolerated.

After 2002, over a patch of time, Sachin had started batting defensively. Vasoo asked me to convey the following message to Sachin: 'The batsman who has abundant strokes in his armour has to play those strokes. Patience, perseverance and stuff like that is not for him.' Sachin laughed heartily when I told this to him.

Despite not having played international cricket, Vasoo knows the game extremely well, and his knowledge is deeper and sounder than that of international cricketers. He is no slave to technique. He once candidly remarked that had

Ajit Wadekar not got mixed up with technique, he would have scored many more runs in Test cricket. Vasoo doesn't care about defensive cricket. He likes the aggressive, Aussie way of playing. While discussing Virender Sehwag on one occasion, he said, 'Sehwag bats as though he doesn't know that a batsman can get out.' In one match, Sehwag was in the middle but the run rate steadily dropped because the batsman at the other end was not scoring. Vasoo's classic observation was, 'If the batsman at one end is batting with the handbrake on and the batsman at the other end is pressing on the accelerator, how will the car run?'

The Generous Genius

Ed Smith

(English author, journalist and former cricketer)

Vasoo would walk all around the net at the Cricket Club of India in Mumbai. He watched from behind the bowler's arm; he watched from square leg; then he watched from behind the stumps.

'Tell me,' he once said to me. 'How many double-hundreds do you have? First-class doubles.' I first recall his tone; the words come to me later. The tone was curious, energetic, engaged, very kindly but also slightly baffled, as though something didn't add up. It was the runs, the doubles—that's what didn't add up.

'None? Really, none at all? But why? Why not? What's the problem?'

Vasoo sets the bar very high for batsmanship. He recognizes talent, nurtures talent, encourages talent. But there is a flip side—there are the things that come bound up with Vasu's support. He expects players to aim high. In the gentlest way, he expects players to push themselves, to go past what they are settling for and aim to be the player they might become one day.

I'd already had a few cycles of form in my career. A fast start, an early dip. Now, I was finding my voice again. I was twenty-five and visiting India to experience cricket through a new lens. Where better than Mumbai? It has a special tradition of batsmanship: Manjrekar, Gavaskar, Tendulkar and all the rest.

When you spoke to men such as Vasoo and Hanumant Singh, you entered a much wider conversation. It was just a chat on one level. But it was also an exposure to the vast accumulated wisdom and expertise of a brilliant cricketing culture. The advice and observations—which influenced me deeply—were only the tip of a much greater body of knowledge. These men sought to understand the full art of batsmanship—to capture its traditions and truths—then pass it on to the next generation. Masters who wanted to share their mastery with others.

Vasoo said very little to me about technique. But he did once look at my batting stance and advised, 'Too hunched. Try a long handle.' I did, and never returned to short-handle bats.

When he demonstrated shots, I sensed in him a reverence for skill, craft and control. Conversations with Vasoo always left me feeling the same way. On the one hand, I longed for more skill, more mastery in my own game; on the other hand, I felt that those things were not out of reach. Yes, the bar was higher, but I felt taller. Great teachers set the goal only just out of reach: not too far to be daunting, not so close as to be easy. When I returned home that season, I got two double-hundreds and played a little for England.

When I think of Vasoo, I remember the voice of a true teacher, and the quest for mastery he sends his students on—something that extends into many spheres, far beyond the dusty boundary edges of cricket fields in India, and endures long after the long handles have been put away in the attic.

An Encyclopedia of Cricket

Milind Rege

(Former Mumbai captain and chief selector)

What has the name Vasoo Paranjape meant to a generation of cricketers for the past fifty years? Respect, integrity, loyalty, charm, class. His name makes us think of his respect for the game, his deep knowledge of the game, his leadership, his dapper appearance. But above all, his name evokes in all of us—across generations—love for the man.

I first saw Vasoo when I was eleven years old, at a Police Shield final between the mighty ACC (Associated Cement Companies) and the giants of club cricket Dadar Union. The year was 1960. Vasoo scored a brilliant century against the might of Ramakant Desai, Polly Umrigar and Bapu Nadkarni to name a few. That innings is still etched in my memory all these decades later. I took to Vasoo immediately! I wanted to be closer to him, see him, follow him everywhere. Little did I realize that five years later, when I would turn into a sixteen-

year-old spring chicken, he would take me under his wing
to teach me the nuances of this great game, in fact teach me
how to play the game.

I was a fast learner. I did everything Vasoo taught me,
not because I was a great student but because the teacher was
so brilliant. I called him what the average Bombay cricketer
would call their seniors, 'Sir'. But he put me at ease. Vasoo
Sir became Vasoo and the ice was broken.

He had this great knack of nicknaming us. Sunil became
Sunny, Milind became Minky and so on. Dadar Union
had become a family to us. On every occasion that we met
before the start of a game, Sunil and I would flock around
Vasoo and pick his brains as to what the combination of the
team would be, and he would explain to us how a team was
compiled.

When Vasoo took over as captain, it was a fun time at
DU. The days of stern faces, scared looks were a thing of
the past. 'Enjoy your day' was our new credo. When a Kanga
League game was washed out, what concerned us wasn't so
much missing the game as missing a chance to meet Vasoo.
Such was his magnetic presence, and such was our affection
for Vasoo.

So thorough was his knowledge of the game that he
was the cynosure of all cricketing parties. Vasoo could
take on a Garfield Sobers and tell him about every run
he had scored. If anyone wanted to hear about Sir Don
Bradman's greatness, Vasoo was an encyclopedia on the
subject. He can rattle off stats from all the performances
of the great man.

Vasoo's sense of humour and his ready wit are unparalleled. Once, I was going through a gruelling spell for Dadar Union and, after a point, I wanted to be relieved. Vasoo very lovingly put his arm around my shoulder and cajoled me to continue. 'Vasoo,' I told him, 'it's too hot.' 'Not to worry, Minky. I shall solve your problem.' And guess what he did? He called out to Lakhandar, our helper, and asked him to bring an umbrella. The team was wondering what our skipper was up to! Vasoo gave me the parasol and asked me to bowl with it. 'You will feel cooler under the shade,' he said. It was the funniest moment of my life. We loved him for his humour. And we loved him as captain, coach, mentor. He was brilliant in all these roles, but above all he was—is—a beautiful person.

When I became a Mumbai selector, I always sought his guidance. 'When you select a player, Minky,' he once said, 'allow him to fail. Only then should you decide his future.' I still follow that advice to a T.

Vasoo set me up for life. He picked me to join Tata Sports Club, and so all my early days were spent under his tutelage. He was the most brilliant captain I have known, along with our Mumbai captain Ajit Wadekar.

These days, when we all meet, we always flock around Vasoo, listening to his unending anecdotes and laughing all the way. I go home happy, and that's what dear Vasoo is all about. He brings happiness to those around him and to so many more.

And Lalita stands like a rock behind Vasoo. She has taken care of all of us, through those countless lunches at her Matunga home through all those years of DU cricket. Thank you, Lalita, for taking care of us. Without you, Dadar Union would not have been the same team. I remember how we laughed, cried and shared our emotions. And these memories we will cherish all our lives. God bless you both and thank you for being there!

Talking Vasoo

Darshak Mehta

*(Chairman, LBW Fund, Sydney,
and Vasoo's former student)*

For about twenty-five years, if there was a rain delay in Kanga League matches during Bombay's monsoon season, club cricketers had to pass their time doing various things in their tents: playing cards, gossiping, napping and talking Vasoo.

Talking Vasoo?

Well, if there was one legend in the maidans of Bombay, between about 1970 and 1995, it was the highly charismatic Vasoo Paranjape. His wisecracks brought many a tent down. From Sunil Gavaskar to Dilip Vengsarkar, from Ravi Shastri to Sanjay Manjrekar and tens of others—each had a favourite Vasoo story. And, these worthies took great delight in telling their stories.

Even if one had heard these several times before, the stories were still compelling. The gags and punchlines were just as funny the ninth time around as they had been when they were first told. And everyone swore the stories were true.

But to speak of Vasoo as merely a glib entertainer would be silly. He could talk, sure. He was invariably funny, of course. He was quick-witted, absolutely. But one could rarely win a cricketing argument with Vasoo. He would overwhelm you with anecdotes and overpower you with facts and statistics. He would also contextualize his arguments using data related to match conditions, opposition attack, wicket quality, etc.

All my past meetings and conversations with him were simply glorious. I have known him for about forty-five years and even today, when talking to him, I have to be at the top of my game and be fully engaged, otherwise he makes mincemeat of me.

Vasoo was the most influential man in my life. Not just cricket-wise but in other matters too. I tried to emulate his talking style, his irreverent humour, his devastating and sardonic wit, and much more. I rarely succeeded in doing so, but it was a winning formula in that it gave me a lot of confidence when it came to interacting with people. Using humour to disarm or amuse and sometImes even distract is a gift, and Vasoo is a wizard at it!

I'd like to share a famous Vasoo story. It concerns Ramnath Kenny and Vasoo during a Ranji match in which Vasoo was the twelfth man. He was run ragged by Kenny's demands: 'Get me a glass of water'; 'I'd like a cup of tea'; 'Is there a sandwich available?' etc., etc. After one too many such demands, Vasoo ran out to the middle with a menu card and told Kenny that it would be easier if he could let him know exactly what his lordship prefers. Both the teams and the umpires were in splits!

I met Vasoo for the first time in 1974, when I went to our Sydenham College nets one afternoon. After bowling for about half an hour in the sun I'd had enough and gave the ball to someone else. But Vasoo would have none of it—he told me that I needed to bowl from the start of the training session, at 3.30 p.m., to the finish, at 5.30 p.m. No ifs, no buts.

Consequently, I did get a taste of bowling long spells and learnt how to develop patience. As a leggie, I used to bowl what I thought was an aggressive line: leg stump and outside. He told me to stop, as by sticking to this line I was taking the LBW out of play. Besides, not many top-class batsmen would get bowled sweeping or behind the legs. So I tightened up and began bowling middle and leg, and I never forgot that lesson.

Another thing he told me after seeing me bamboozle (but not get out) some tailender was that I should never try to get tailenders out or bowl differently to them. 'Darshak, why commit murder when a man is hell-bent on suicide?' I never forgot that one either.

His coaching style was totally unobtrusive and non-judgemental. He tried to get cricketers to think and strive to become the best they could be. He was easily the most successful club captain that Bombay has ever had—aggressive, confident and without a defensive bone in him. You felt ten feet tall and five feet wide when you played for him, as I did when, on the odd occasion, I turned out for Dadar Union.

One of the greatest compliments he paid me was when he said to me, in 1978 (I even remember where), that he had no doubt that if I were an Australian, I would have played for Australia as a leg-spinner, since I was a better leggie than Peter Sleep, who was the main Australian leg-spinner back then. Anyway, I took that as a compliment to me rather than as a withering assessment of Sleep—which it probably was!

I used to visit 'Sir', as I still call him, and Lalita Aunty at their home every few months and passively inhale smoke (he was a compulsive smoker in those days—about forty cigarettes a day) while shooting the breeze on his balcony. He would use a flower pot (with a small plant in it) as his ashtray and drive Lalita Aunty mad! We would talk cricket, watch international games, discuss the legends of the game, and he would relate one funny episode after another. Before I knew it, I had been there for three or four hours. Jatin was very young then, and he undoubtedly grew up on a diet of cricket history. I am not quite sure what he makes of the fact that I meet so many of the legends of the game that he admired and spoke about in hushed tones: Lillee, Ian Chappell, Greg Chappell, etc. One of my greatest personal thrills was to be asked by Greg Chappell, a childhood idol of mine, to write the foreword to his autobiography. I have yet to recover from that and consequently have an ego bigger than Brazil.

In conclusion, I must relate another *real* story, from 2001. It happened in Calcutta. I was in the Australian dressing room and Vasoo rang when India were bowled out cheaply. He asked me if we (Australia) were enforcing the follow-on. I said, yes we were. He literally screamed and told me to go up to Buchanan (the coach) and Steve Waugh (the captain) and tell them that it was a great mistake they were making. They had their foot on India's neck and by enforcing the follow-on, they were allowing India back in the game, he thought. Remember, we are talking about one of the greatest and strongest teams of all time, Waugh's team, which until then had won sixteen-odd Tests consecutively. I told him that I had absolutely no 'locus standi' on telling the team what to do or advising them on cricket tactics. I wish I had! Vasoo, of course, turned out to be prophetic. He saw and predicted what no one else could. Till today, teams all over the world are reluctant to enforce follow-ons after what happened in Calcutta in 2001.

On the next Australian tour to India, in 2004, Vasoo met Adam Gilchrist and Justin Langer at their request, over dinner at the Taj. I'd organized it. Gilly and JL were extremely keen to pick his brain and questioned him closely on what the Aussies were doing wrong and what they needed to do better. Vasoo's tips went a long, long way in helping Australia finally win a series in India. Every other day of the series, Gilly used to ask me what the 'great man' thought about their game.

Well, what can I say? The great man is a guru not only to me but to tens of others like me. We have learnt so much from him, not just about how to play cricket but about how to lead our lives better.

'Sir' is unique. He is a character. God simply threw away the die after making him.

Remembering the 1987 World Cup

Vijay Lokapally

(Author and journalist)

'**A**rré second slip *ghe*, second slip (bring in second slip).'
Vasoo Paranjape was agitated. He was not on the field
but watching the game from a quiet corner. He had been
talking to some of us, but his eyes were glued to the middle.
His mind and eyes had struck a perfect balance between
us and the contest. He was not going to miss the action.
And what happened on the next ball was astonishing. The
batsman edged the ball precisely into the vacant area he had
referred to—the second slip. His response was a disappointed
glance at us, and in that one moment I discovered the astute
cricketing brain of Vasoo Sir.

One had heard tales about his cricket acumen from
former Test players, including some Mumbai stalwarts; and
of course, from cricket scribes and other beneficiaries of his
guidance. Nothing could distract Vasoo Sir from his love of
the game. Nothing. 'Cricket is my life,' he would say, never

failing to remind us that this great game was the elixir for him. I don't think there has ever been a day in his life that went by without him uttering the word 'cricket' at least a hundred times.

I had met him a few times in Bombay back in the day, with my friend Dwarkanath Sanzgiri. But it was during the 1987 Reliance World Cup camp for Indian probables that I got introduced to this wonderful cricket guru. My daily visits to the National Stadium in Delhi, where he was appointed as a coach along with Captain K.B. Dogra, were no less than a cricket pilgrimage.

The camp had the cream of Indian cricket: twenty-five hand-picked players preparing for the upcoming World Cup. Sunil Gavaskar, Kapil Dev, Dilip Vengsarkar, Ravi Shastri were some of the big names at this camp, which had been shifted to Delhi from Udaipur because the administration was unhappy with the quality of pitches at Udaipur.

'The fitness is tested during the last ten overs or so. It is a question of anticipation and speed, mental and physical. How you synchronize these becomes important then,' Vasoo Sir said at that time in an interview to *Sportstar* magazine. What he observed in 1987 holds true in every format of the game in contemporary cricket.

I was awestruck by how Vasoo Sir commanded respect from the stars of Indian cricket. They would stand in rapt attention whenever he spoke, and there was a lot of banter and laughter too. With Vasoo Sir around, the discussions about the game were never too serious or boring. He would lighten up the conversation with his delightful anecdotes.

He always had an anecdote to drive home a point, and the cricketers loved every moment of it.

Vasoo Sir concentrated on fielding drills and net sessions. His sessions in 1987 were aimed at getting the players into the right frame of mind before the World Cup started. He would work for an hour or so with Laxman Sivaramakrishnan daily. 'He has tremendous cricket knowledge, and I can't think of a greater motivator,' said Sivaramakrishnan, recalling that camp. Vasoo Sir made two great predictions at that camp: 'Watch out for John Emburey and Navjot Singh Sidhu.' Emburey played all eight matches for England and finished with the best economy rate among the regular bowlers. Sidhu? He was the revelation of the tournament.

Sidhu had played just two Test matches before he was picked for the Reliance World Cup camp and was regarded as a 'defensive' batsman by most critics. One scribe had called him a 'strokeless wonder'. And yet, Vasoo Sir wanted us to believe that this Punjab opener was the one to watch in the Indian team. It was hard to accept this. But then you don't question Vasoo Sir, do you?

In an interview to my colleague K.P. Mohan, even before the Indian team had been picked, Vasu Sir has said about Sidhu, 'He has played some stupendous shots at the nets. He seems to have hidden a lot of his stroke-making talent, which he is unravelling now.' When I probed him further on this, Vasoo Sir observed, 'He [Sidhu] is in tremendous nick. His timing of the ball, literally no edges flying off his bat, very few balls hitting his pads—all this convinces me that he is going to be a consistent scorer. The sound of the bat meeting the ball is so sweet when Sherry is batting.' Vasoo

Sir was spot on. Sidhu batted five times in that tournament and scored 73, 75, 51, 55, 22—in that sequence.

Over the years, it has been my privilege to be able to interact with Vasoo Sir. 'Are you in Mumbai?' would be his warm remark whenever I would call him. 'I don't like speaking on the phone much,' he would say. 'When are you coming?' The distance between Delhi and Mumbai hindered the possibility of frequent meetings with Vasoo Sir. But he has always been a phone call away, ready to regale us with his cricket anecdotes and priceless wisdom, which made us understand the game better.

Cricket's Simple Logician

Rahul Mankad

(Former Mumbai batsman, and son of cricketer Vinoo Mankad)

I was fortunate to have been introduced to Mr Paranjape when I was very young. He was my father's favourite, because Vinoobhai found Vasoo Uncle's enthusiasm and love for the game genuine. There was an amazing curiosity and a fierce desire in him to learn the intricacies of the game rather than a fascination for statistics. I remember Vinoobhai telling me to spend time with his favourite friend as he had a lot to offer to up-and-coming young players.

Vasoo Uncle's biggest strength was his ability to relate to a player and understand the challenges he faced as a cricketer. He coached with great passion and ensured his message got home by making his explanations less complicated, shedding all kinds of jargon and using simple language and logic.

I was prone to getting bowled out early in my career and sought advice and counsel from Vasoo Uncle. He watched me for a while and told me that there wasn't much wrong with the way I was approaching batting as my mindset was positive. He then gave me a simple but excellent pointer by suggesting that I should ensure that my back elbow (the right elbow as I was a right-hander) brushes my side every time played the ball. This resulted in my bat coming down straight, negating the gap between bat and body. A simple but very effective tip. This is one example of how observant he was and how he could offer simple solutions to problems faced by young batsmen.

Vasoo Uncle's great attribute was his positivity and his positive outlook on cricket. He was influenced tremendously by watching, reading about and following the greats of his time, such as Bradman, Sobers, Vinoo Mankad and Frank Worrell. They were all aggressive and positive and never took a step back when playing the game. His message as a coach all along was to be positive and always approach the game with the mindset to dominate, whether batting or bowling. He was our manager/coach at Nirlon, and he was a great observer and sounding board to us, as well as a very harsh critic of mediocrity and lack of intensity. We became a stronger unit because of him.

I also played against him in the Mumbai inter-club matches, and he always played hard and very fair; he hated losing, but he was always gracious after the game. He influenced many young and aspiring cricketers and taught them how the game ought to be played.

The best advice he gave me was, 'Don't just be a cricket player. Be a *cricketer*. Embody this spirit and live the game through your life.' This has stood me in good stead throughout my life. Great words of wisdom from a great coach and a great man.

Musings on Cricket*

Vasoo Paranjape

A Vacation for Consistency

Now that the selection of the Indian team has been made and soon they will get together at Bangalore for the camp, one wonders what qualities the selectors expect from the players.

It should be consistency on all counts that they must be expecting. But somehow, it is the same thing—consistency—that one finds missing totally when it comes to the selection.

What a player has to his credit is known to almost all, but what he is capable of producing tomorrow should be more important than anything else. Potential and temperament should be the factors that the selectors should worry about more than the runs scored and wickets taken against a particular opposition.

---

* The pieces collected in this chapter first appeared, in a slightly different form, in *The Hindu*, for which Vasoo Paranjape wrote a cricket column in 1979.

The present selection is quite unconvincing, unimaginative, inconsistent and lopsided. Five bowlers, two wicketkeepers and nine batsmen are what we have got in this team. Chandrasekhar and Chetan Chauhan will join the team later. For the Prudential Cup. We have to use at least three of the five bowlers unless Venkataraghavan* asks Mohinder, Yajurvindra Singh and Gaekwad to manage 12 overs each. To bowl 12 overs against the West Indians will not be easy.

In case these so-called all-rounders do that, still the very important job of getting the opponent out—a possibility that should not be overlooked—will depend on total luck. Since Gaekwad is selected ahead of Chauhan, one wonders if the selectors have also considered Gaekwad as a bowler. I am sure they must have a cause. Gaekwad is more strokeless than he was in the past.

Our regular bowlers will be Venkataraghavan, Karsan Ghavri, Kapil Dev and Bishan Singh Bedi. Any one of them getting unfit and the attack can hardly be formidable. Sunil Valson, Dhiraj Parsana and M.V. Narasimha Rao would have provided some relief if not the edge and variety. For a tour of England, albeit a short one, having two regular opening bowlers is far from a satisfactory provision. Valson may not shake England with his pace but would have come back with more knowledge of the business than he can acquire in his entire life in North Zone cricket and on North Zone wickets.

Parsana may not be in the same class to replace Bedi but with his utility as a two-in-one bowler, he would have kept

---

* S. Venkataraghavan was the captain of the Indian team for this series.

the regulars fresh for the Tests. Yashpal Sharma could not replace the out-of-form Mohinder on the placid Pakistan pitches. Can one expect him to do it in England?

Surinder Khanna replacing the seasoned Kirmani and not replacing the untried Bharat Reddy is the biggest shock. The man who should have accompanied Kirmani is Zulfiqar Parkar. A keeper's main job in Test cricket is his work behind the stumps, and his work in front should be a bonus for the team.

Only one pair of opening bowlers to England is most unconvincing. They may have to be brought into the attack on more than one occasion during the day's play. And with nobody to relieve them in the succeeding matches, their plight can be pitiable.

The Tricky Tour Ahead

In a few months, India will tour England to play a Test series and will also participate in the second World Cup. Selecting a touring party has always been a favourite pastime of cricket buffs, and I guess I am no exception. Some countries have decided to recall players earlier for the World Cup, to strengthen the team or to have full representation. We have no such ticklish problems. However, selecting the right team to face English conditions has always been difficult for us, as English conditions are variable, sometimes even during the day's play.

I have not been to England and have not experienced the conditions personally, but from whatever I have gathered from the English press and from former Indian players,

I would go for the following Indian lineup: Gavaskar, Venkataraghavan, Chauhan, Mohinder Amarnath, Dilip Vengsarkar, Gundappa Viswanath, Brijesh Patel, Yajurvindra Singh, Syed Kirmani, Bharath Reddy, Kapil Dev, Karsan Ghavri, Pandurang Salgaonkar, Sunil Valson, Narasimha Rao and Dhiraj Parsana.

This team is almost new to English conditions. Barring Gavaskar, Viswanath and Brijesh Patel, none of the others have faced English bowling in English conditions on English wickets. More than anything else, the climatic conditions have taken a toll on most visiting teams in the past. We will have to tackle this aspect with whatever material available on hand. Just because one does not have top-class fast bowlers, one cannot use the best spinners—may be even the best in the world—on green wickets and then expect a convincing performance. Fast bowlers on the Swansea track and spinners on the Lord's track can hardly produce the desired results.

These are my thoughts on the Indian team:

Gavaskar: At present, he must be the best opener in the world. Unless he opts to drop the mantle of captaincy, he should lead India.

Venkataraghavan: Whenever called upon to do the duty, he has invariably shouldered it convincingly.

Chauhan: Should continue to open with Gavaskar but may find himself out of the team during the limited-overs World Cup matches.

Vengsarkar: In spite of the two centuries, he is not exuding enough confidence. Predetermined in his initial movements. Hence commits himself early to a shot and finds himself either inside or outside the line of the ball. Should get over this self-made problem. May have to open during the World Cup matches. Always a better opening player when stroking the ball.

Viswanath: Superb player on all counts and in all situations but showing signs of slowing down in his reflexes on the field.

Mohinder Amarnath: Only a season ago, he was hailed by teammates as the best player. Unlucky to get the axe after the first Test. Capable of opening the innings because of his temperament. He is unsteady only when facing short-pitched stuff.

Brijesh Patel: Dislikes the fast stuff more than others. Once settled down, he can win a match on his own, and as a fielder he is superb.

Yajurvindra Singh: Talented stroke player. With patience and application, he should be able to come back home as a reliable middle-order batsman. Has an excellent record as a close-to-the-wicket catcher. Can relieve the bowling for a while.

Kirmani: May have suffered a bad patch in between, but an able keeper and a great team man. Can be trusted in critical situations to get runs. Has done enough to prove himself.

Bharat Reddy: Has not got the chance to prove his potential. Has been in the Test atmosphere for quite some time. Zulfiqar Parkar of Bombay must be very close on his heels to make the grade. Second keeper of the team, mainly because he has been on the Test scene for some time.

Kapil Dev: Has emerged as a top-class all-rounder. Full of life, whether batting, bowling or fielding. A tour of England will help him tremendously.

Ghavri: Has done extremely well with the bat and the ball. Can run into trouble when bowling slow stuff. Has come to stay for some time.

Salgaonkar: Totally overlooked after his Sri Lanka tour. Should be one of the quickest in the country. Needs to get himself in better shape. Should be able to more than relieve the main pair of opening bowlers. Has to be handled well.

Sunil Valson: Can be groomed into a Test-class bowler. Should have been an automatic choice for the President's XI game against the West Indians. Very keen and hard-working cricketer.

Narasimha Rao: Must be the only leg-spinner to bowl a fair number of overs regularly in Ranji Trophy matches. This type matures late. He needs to be groomed into a Test-class player.

Dhiraj Parsana: Over the years he has performed in Ranji cricket. Played in Tests either on unsuitable wickets or in unsuitable situations. Gritty bowler who can bowl with the new one and for long spells, as well as with the old one. Should prove very useful on the tour.

If the Board decides to send seventeen players instead of sixteen, I would send Surinder Amarnath to fit the number-three spot in the batting lineup for the World Cup. A camp to condition the players and a plan to reach England ten days ahead of the schedule should be helpful to get the players acclimatized.

Are Our Spinners over the Hill?

This great game of cricket is dominated by the batsmen to such an extent that most marathon bowling performances are almost totally forgotten by most people. Only the other day, a boiling performance of 5 for 116 off 43 overs by Chandrasekhar was forgotten because of two memorable batting displays by Sunil Gavaskar and Alvin Kallicharran.

One wonders why cricket is a batsman's game. One reason, perhaps the most important, is that the batsman, no matter how great, has only one chance technically. (Maybe a statistician can establish the point using previous records that on an average, every batsman gets a certain number of lives per innings.) As against this, the bowler has at least six chances to prove himself.

Let us forget the extreme possibility of a no-ball fetching a run-out, though I have seen a pair of Test players separated by the above sequence. So this is not far-fetched; it is one of those uncertainties of this game.

The attention and praise that a batsman gets is quite often not justified. More so if he belongs to the visitors. In the first Test at the Wankhede Stadium, Bombay, Kallicharran scored 187, but his 100-plus on Sunday and the subsequent 80-plus on Tuesday were so distinctly different that one wondered whether it was the same batsman.

After about two frustrating hours of inconsistent timing, he threw away his bat and also kicked it in total disgust. This was enough to show his displeasure with his own form during that particular patch.

During this spell of two hours and more, Chandrasekhar and Bedi were trying every trick known to them, but the edges and the mishits resulted in nothing at all. But that is the way it goes.

Poor Venkataraghavan and Bedi must have wondered about the returns they got from this wicket, which gradually did become slow but turned quite alarmingly towards the end. One was confronted with the question: What might have happened had the four hours not been lost on the first day of the match?

Elsewhere, it is regular practice to make good the loss of time on subsequent days of play. Had this been done, the West Indians could have found our spinners during the last phase of the match a totally different proposition. Our spinning trio might then have answered the question some sports scribes are asking perhaps a bit too early: 'Are our spinners over the hill?'

Fighters to the Last

The Aussies are here. Though the Indians will be following them in a fortnight's time, not all the Indian players are likely to be as fresh and raring to go as the visitors.

The Australians traditionally are a brand of cricketers who are highly confident, almost to the point of arrogance, with attack as their main approach in a tight situation. Coupled with their true killer instinct is the Australians' almost fanatical belief that no game is lost till the last ball is bowled. Their fielding-oriented approach enables them to fight to the last. With the interference of Kerry Packer, the Australian team has weakened to a great extent. Though Ian and Greg Chappell, Lillee and Jeff Thomson are not going to be among the visitors, the bowling department of the present team is comparatively stronger than its batting.

Though Rodney Hogg, Alan Hurst and company will not find the Indian surfaces to their liking—with the possible exception of Madras and probably Eden Gardens—the batting lineup of Graeme Wood, Rick Darling, Kim Hughes, Graham Yallop and Allan Border is certainly going to put up improved performances as the series progresses.

What, then, should be our line of thinking to beat the Australians?

Our selectors should take a positive and progressive approach of blending the team with a proper mixture of spinners and pacemen. As the present Indian spinning trio is showing signs of decline, this department needs to be rejuvenated. Moreover, as the visitors have shown a long-standing weakness against spin, particularly off spin, the Indian lineup of spinners should be off-spin-oriented, with even two off-spinners if necessary. The spinners will not be successful unless supported by razor-sharp fielding, which can also enable the Indians to exploit the chink in the Aussie cricket armour: their present frequency of run-outs at international levels, with Wood being the chief offender in this respect.

Why Not Ex-players as Umpires?

One of the most thankless jobs in cricket, I feel, is that of the wicketkeeper. Even after he takes part in five dismissals behind the wickets, 'the one that got away' is invariably the point of discussion in the evening.

But have you ever given a thought to the job of the umpire? Well, his job not only beats the wicketkeeper's hands down as being the most thankless, but as a matter of fact the umpire is the subject of lengthier discussions at the camp.

I feel sorry for the poor person. Can one ensure absolute perfection in this ever-vulnerable job? No, none can gain a 100 per cent result, but one can certainly move towards this target. I feel that former first-class players with experience of about twenty-five matches behind them, or ex-Test players with similar experience, can surely play some part towards achieving this target. At present, most umpires in England are former players and their standard of umpiring is widely accepted as the best all over the world. I am not trying to convey that our first-class umpires have no experience of playing, but continuous exposure to first-class cricket that makes a player battle-scarred is what the umpire needs to see himself through the most critical situations. The experience of their playing days helps them to read 'straight throughs' and arm balls better and makes their response to these deliveries more knowledgeable.

Former players as umpires will certainly tackle problems more smoothly than others. Problems like padding-up outside the off stump, left-hander bowling over the wicket, hit wicket while hooking or sweeping, bad-light stoppages. Interpretations in such situations will be more acceptable to players when done by umpires with playing experience behind them.

Let us weigh some more tricky situations. An umpire known for ruling 'not out' when the batsman plays forward is often later taken for a ride by a clever batsman. How often does Chandrasekhar turn his leg break that a batsman playing forward should not be declared out LBW? This applies all the more to our wickets, which are known for their lack of bounce. A former leg-spinner as umpire would understand this situation best.

Exactly the other way round would be the case when Erapalli Prasanna is bowling on a turning wicket to a clever batsman, who is playing forward outside the line of the off stump and allowing the delivery to hit the front foot by merely pretending to play. The intention of the batsman will be judged better by ex-players as umpires. Their interpretation of cricketing laws will be more in keeping with the spirit rather than the letter.

Now, with remuneration being handsome and the frequency of Test matches fairly high, what is holding up the ex-player from coming out to the middle again, not in cream flannels but in a white coat? I feel that umpiring decisions made at all stages of the game will become more acceptable if the umpires had playing experience. That is why I am appealing to ex-players to don the white coat.

Epilogue: The Dadar Union Family

There are some people who are under the mistaken impression that Dadar Union is a cricket club. Nestled in a corner of Matunga in Mumbai, this institution was so revered that it was believed that once you received your Dadar Union cap, it was only a matter of time before you played for Bombay and, obviously, for India. But Dadar Union is neither a club nor a venue; it's neither a breeding ground for cricketers nor a stepping stone to better things. It is a way of life.

Let's start with its most illustrious product, Sunil Gavaskar, who once returned to Bombay after a stint for Somerset in England and was ready to pad up for Dadar Union within hours. 'I am not sure whether I wanted to play more for Dadar Union or for India,' Gavaskar said back then. 'Dadar Union taught me to respect the game, to value tradition, to be disciplined and have a direction in cricket. Without Dadar Union, I would never have become the player I did.' That's Gavaskar, with 10,122 Test runs behind him, the first man to breach the five-figure mark and arguably the most technically adept player the country has ever produced.

But a bit of history first. Established in 1927, Dadar Union had to wait till 1951 to top the charts in the Kanga League, beating longtime rivals Jolly Cricketers. Madhav Mantri steered the club towards better times and they came out on top in 1958 and 1959. But it was in the 1970s that Dadar Union really became a force to reckon with.

Between 1973 and 1976, Dadar Union dominated the domestic leagues, not allowing any other team to come close to taking top honours. And in all these years it was led by Vasoo Paranjape. During this golden era, Dadar Union also won the Purshottam Shield and the Talim Shield five years on the trot and secured the Comrade Shield for nine consecutive years.

There is a classic example of the Dadar Union spirit from the 1974 season, when they were playing against a Bombay University team that boasted Dilip Vengsarkar, Sandeep Patil, Suru Nayak and Vijay Mohanraj. Dadar Union were in trouble at 92 for 5, but at that point Vasoo, to the mystification of all, declared the innings. Avadhut Zarapkar, a former Dadar Union player who had turned out for the University team at that time, recalls the disbelief all around. 'I remember Sandeep [Patil] asking whether Vasoo thought we were a *popatwadi* [pushover] team. We were soon to find out. Urmikant Mody and Vithal Patil took five apiece to dismiss us for 55.'

Vasoo, as always, had a very simple explanation. 'There was a match to be won,' he said. 'If our team, which included a certain Sunil Gavaskar, found it so difficult to score, then the opposition would struggle too.'

This is the Dadar Union spirit as embodied by Vasoo Paranjape. The badge on the Dadar Union cap reads, 'Union is Strength'. But it could well have read, 'A Temple of Learning'. As Dilip Vengsarkar, another famous alumnus, puts it: 'In Dadar Union, everything was planned and implemented thoroughly. Every Saturday we would practise. Vasoo Paranjape was a great motivator and more than that, a terrific captain. If he could not get the best out of a player through commonsense, he would do it with wit.'

So without further ado, here's Vasoo on what Dadar Union was all about. 'There used to be a big tradition of club cricket in Bombay. And I think every member of each club took great pride in playing for their clubs and continued to play for the clubs even after having played Ranji later on. So, the value of club cricket was very high. And I very distinctly remember going and watching senior cricket matches instead of playing junior cricket, just to get a better feel of things to come.'

Wait, what? He used to go and watch matches rather than playing and trying to force his case?

'You know, all the big guys were playing for Dadar Union,' recalls Vasoo. '[Madhav] Mantri was the captain and almost everybody was a Ranji Trophy player in that particular team. And everybody concentrated so hard that if you didn't do well, you were likely to be left out. In my first year, 1953, I was only in the reserves. I was only about fourteen or fifteen at the time. But I used to love fielding and I made sure I was good at it, so that they always made me the twelfth man. I became the permanent twelfth man, and slowly things fell into place.'

Back in the day, one didn't actually get any money playing for a prestigious club like Dadar Union. 'There was zero money,' Vasoo says. 'But, luckily for us, there were also reasonably tolerable expenses when it came to running a club. Apart from preparing a wicket, you had a *bhaiyya* who was supposed to be a groundsman. Only he knew what he was doing, and everybody simply came and played there.'

The reason you turned out for Dadar Union was prestige. 'Look, back in those days there were some things you learnt from coaches—like your basic technique, how to approach batting or bowling—but beyond that you picked up all the finer points from playing matches and watching your seniors,' says Vasoo. 'At Dadar Union, the first thing you learnt was discipline. It did not matter how big a name you were. Whether you were playing for India at the time or in your first season of club cricket, the same rules applied to everyone. If you were late in reporting to the ground for a match, you expected to be dropped. There would be no discussion, even if a junior had to be picked in place of the main batsman. The second thing you learnt at Dadar Union was that it was not only about runs and wickets. There was a certain way to play the game. You show the game respect and it will take care of you. You monkey around, and that's it, you're gone.'

One of the great bonds that Vasoo formed at Dadar Union, while captaining the team for three decades starting 1966, was with Gavaskar. 'Talking to Sunny was never a problem,' he says. 'Whether it was at my house before a match, over a cup of tea, or out on the street near my car, where we would bump into each other sometimes, or at the ground—it was never difficult to communicate with Sunny. When it came to batting, there was hardly anything you needed to tell Sunny. He was the kind of player and person who was so conscious about his own technique that he was always thinking about it. If his bat was not coming down straight, nobody needed to point it out to him. He knew right away what was wrong. Where I would sometimes step in was in giving him the confidence to rectify this in the shortest period of time. And Sunny loved to talk about the game—about the tactics, the approach to different situations. So, naturally, it was always easy for us to be in each other's company.'

From Madhav Mantri to Gavaskar, from Dilip Vengsarkar to Sanjay Manjrekar, Dadar Union's pantheon of players is too exhaustive to list here. That would take a book of its own. Suffice to say that it was players such as Vasoo who made Dadar Union what it was. 'You know,' he says, 'the only reason I stopped playing for Dadar Union was because Jatin started to play. He was only a little boy but he said to me, "Daddy, if you are still playing I'm not going to play." Then I knew it was time to step away. I stopped playing, but Dadar Union was, is and always will be my club.'

Acknowledgements

I would like to thank my father for going down memory lane and patiently answering all my questions. It does get tough in one's advancing years. I thank my mother, for being a keen and willing partner during this process, handwriting notes of the conversations as a backup to the audio!

I am grateful to my father's Dadar Union teammates, especially Avi Karnik, Urmikant Modi, Jitu Bhutta, Satya Uncle and the late Dr Mukund Joshi, for recounting several anecdotes; and to Mr Sunil Gavaskar, for writing the foreword to this book and being 'Sunny' to my father for all these years.

To all the cricketers mentioned in this book, a huge thank you for being genuinely encouraging and interested in sharing these stories, so that they can impact young Indians.

A big thank you to my brilliant writer friend Anand Vasu, who has poured all his heart into this book.

I would also like to thank my wife, Gandhali, and my sisters, Radhika and Shubhada.

A big shout out to my friend Sapna Kar (how a conversation turned into a book!); and to Radhika Marwah and Sathya Saran for wanting to tell this coach's story.

Above all, thanks to all of my father's 'students', from the 1970s till now, who, without exception, have only the most gracious things to say about 'Vasoo Sir'.

Mumbai   Jatin Paranjape
June 2020